CAKES

A collection of the
very best baked treats

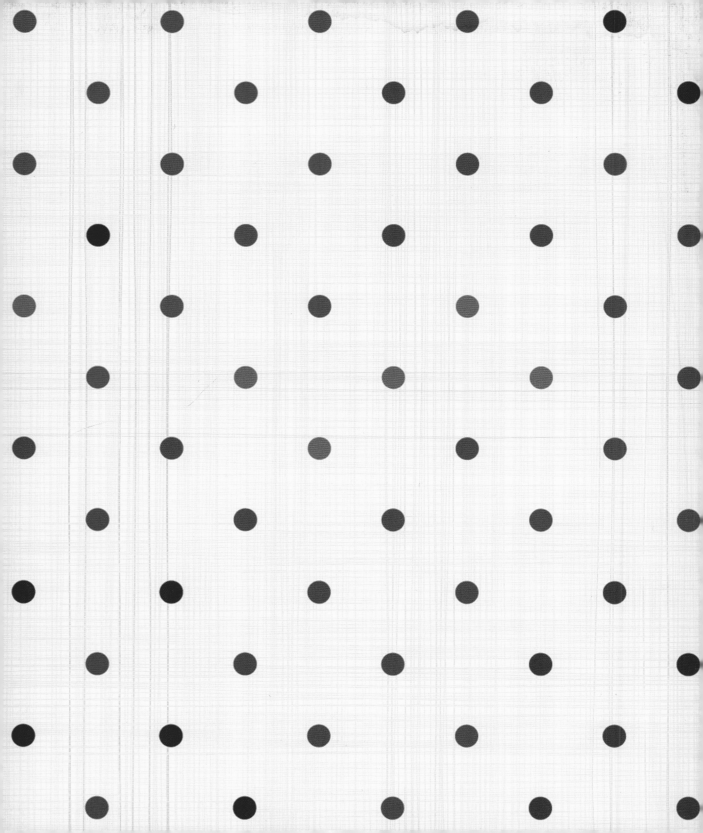

CONTENTS

INTRODUCTION

Amid the stress and chaos of modern life, do you ever long for a few peaceful moments, in which you might do something good and simple and satisfying? As our grandmothers knew, baking a cake is the perfect antidote for worry or ennui. With the right ingredients, a co-operative oven and a touch of skill, anyone can whip up a creation that will dazzle guests, silence a mother-in-law, comfort girlfriends and satisfy a grumbling belly.

This dream compendium of recipes will find you producing ever-more-wonderful treats. Hooray for Nanna's Classics – you will soon be turning out these favourites with astonishing ease. Behold a rich and tasty coffee sandwich cake, best served with gossip; a glorious chocolate cake, dripping in decadence and birthday memories; spicy carrot loaf, topped with thick cream cheese frosting; and many more.

Beyond these beloved originals, we offer a dizzying range of recipes for every possible occasion. The perfection of a simple sponge will delight you, while cheesecakes are arrayed in all their creamy glory, and the full gamut of chocolate cakes are bound to tempt. There are treasures to be discovered among the fruit and nut recipes – familiar walnut and luxurious black forest are just the beginning – and tarts will be crowd-pleasers, whether made with sweet, juicy fruits or eggy, buttery custard.

For snacks, nothing beats a brownie, or a straight-from-heaven slice. And the little ones in your life will be thrilled by your creations on their special days, or just rainy days, made with their imaginations and appetites in mind.

Need a little help to get started? Read our baking advice (page 7) and you'll be up and running in no time. If you measure carefully, and pay attention to your oven's timer and temperature, it's hard to go wrong.

So tie up your apron, take out your mixing bowls and breathe a long, contented sigh. Right now, it's just you, a recipe and the lovely cake to come.

Baking
ADVICE

Helpful hints and trusty tricks

THE BASICS

Most recipe books will dedicate the first chapter to lengthy explanations of cooking terms in order to guarantee sure-fire success. By the time you've made it through the technical information, your enthusiasm is flagging and you're starting to think about a little afternoon nap.

Here, we've tried to distill all you need to know about baking into just a few pages, to avoid boredom or bewilderment. We also want to clarify just how easy it is to bake a cake—it's not rocket science!

Equipment

You don't need expensive equipment. A selection of mixing bowls, wooden spoons and whisks will suffice for preparation of the batter, though if you have an electric mixer, you may find it useful.

If you already have some cake tins, use what you have, but if you are in the market for new ones, choose good quality springform tins. Non-stick tins will give you years of faithful service if you treat them nicely, washing them the old-fashioned way, by hand, and never cutting or scraping them with metal objects.

Preparing your cake tins for the batter is crucial. If a recipe calls for buttering or oiling a cake tin, do so thoroughly, making sure that the entire surface has been buttered. A light dusting of all-purpose flour (plain flour) over the buttered surface will guarantee an easy release of the baked cake (though skip this if a recipe calls for coating the buttered surface with ground nuts, cookie crumbs or coconut).

A surefire way to remove a cake from the base of a springform tin quickly and easily is as follows: before you fill the tin with batter, remove the sides of the tin from the base. Place a large piece of baking paper over the base, then replace the side and close the hinge, creating a tight false bottom on the base. Once the cake has baked and the sides of the tin are removed, place the cake on a platter and slide the tin base out. Then ease the paper out from under the cake and—ta-da!

Quality scales and measuring cups are a necessity. Small, nested sets of cups are useful, as are tablespoon and teaspoon measures. For absolute, care-free ease of measuring, new digital scales can measure liquid, as well as dry ingredients, in imperial and metric measurements.

You will want to make sure that your oven heats accurately. To check, purchase an inexpensive oven thermometer and heat your oven to 400°F (200°C). Place the oven thermometer inside and leave it for 30 minutes. Remove the thermometer and check that it registers within 9°F (5°C). If not, call a serviceman to adjust the oven temperature.

When a recipe calls for toasted nuts or coconut, you can use your handy-dandy microwave if you wish. Spread the nuts onto the glass plate evenly, then cook on high for two minutes. Mix a little, then cook on high additionally as required, one minute at a time, until the nuts or coconut are as golden as you like.

An important note on measurements

As is traditional in baking, for many ingredients, the recipes in this book use spoon and cup measurements. In some cases, for precision, measurements are given in oz and grams.

1 teaspoon = 5g (5ml)

1 tablespoon = 15g (15ml)

Liquid measures: 1 cup = 9 fl oz (250ml).

Solid measures vary depending on the ingredient. For the following key ingredients, they are approximately as follows: 1 cup caster sugar = 7 oz (220g); 1 cup flour = 5oz (150g); 1 cup confectioner's (icing) sugar = 5oz (150g); 1 cup raisins = 5½ oz (170g).

Conversions are rounded for cookery purposes.

Ingredients

The best ingredients are always important. Make sure that your flour is fresh and well-aerated. If you wish to use whole wheat (wholemeal) or rye flour, it is imperative that it is fresh and not rancid. To check, stir a spoonful or two into a glass of warm water. The aroma should be pleasantly floury, not bitter or sour.

Purchase good quality cocoa and chocolate, and store nuts in the freezer so they remain fresher longer. Buy coconut as necessary and make sure that creams, buttermilk and all dairy products are fresh. When using fresh fruit in recipes, ensure they are firm or soft, as the recipe dictates. Using a firm banana where a soft one is called for will change the essence of the recipe.

Many cooks will attempt ambitious dinner menus without batting an eye, yet shake and shudder at the thought of baking a cake. If this is you, please allow us to reassure you—it really isn't very hard, and anyone can do it. We promise.

Some cakes just aren't made for this world. Here's why.

1 Sinking on removal from oven
   a. Too much sugar
   b. Too much raising agent
   c. Removal from oven before completely cooked

2 Soggy base of cake
   a. Ingredients insufficiently blended
   b. Oven temperature too low
   c. Excess moisture
   d. Undercooked

3 Tunnels in cake
   a. Too little shortening in proportion to other ingredients
   b. Over-beating after flour added

4 Cracking of cake
   a. Batter too stiff, insufficient liquid or too much flour
   b. Oven temperature too hot
   c. Restricted surface area of tin

5 Coarse texture

a. Under- or over-beating

b. Too much raising agent

c. Too much sugar

d. Too low cooking temperature

e. Insufficient blending of ingredients

6 Uneven cakes

a. Oven shelf may not be level

b. Cake tin may be uneven

c. Uneven temperature in oven

7 Rising and sinking during baking

a. Too much moisture

b. Too much raising agent

c. Too low oven temperature

d. Too frequent opening of oven door

8 Shrinkage

a. Too much liquid and too little flour

b. Overcooking

9 Poor volume

a. Incorrect measuring of ingredients

b. Excess moisture

HELPFUL HINTS

1 Preheat the oven to the required temperature.

2 Prepare the tins first, as described in the recipe.

3 Have ingredients at room temperature for better mixing.

4 Prepare all ingredients before you start mixing, as a cake batter will lose its lightness if left standing.

5 If the results are to be perfect, do not stop until the cakes are in the oven.

That airy consistency

One essential ingredient in virtually all cakes is delicously light and simple—air.

When vigorously whisked, egg whites capture air bubbles and puff up to many times their original volume. Whether the whisked egg mixture will be folded into a cake batter or whisked with sugar to create meringue, it should be stiff enough to hold its shape.

Yolks or whole eggs whisked over heat with sugar will enfold air and become the basis of a feather-light sponge. You should continue whisking until a trail of mixture falling from the whisk forms a glossy ribbon.

The airy foundation of many sponges and fruit cakes is butter or margarine, beaten with sugar until it changes to a pale shade of cream.

Stiffly whisked egg white

To create the perfect whisked egg whites, separate the eggs carefully—even a trace of yolk will spoil your whites. Put the whites in a large bowl, preferably one made of copper, which reacts chemically with the whites to strengthen the air bubbles. Using a balloon whisk, whisk with a figure-of-eight motion until they begin to foam. Then change to a circular action, whisking until the whites, when lifted on the whisk, hold a peak without the top drooping.

Lining tins for flawless results

Moulds for small cakes need no more preparation than a film of butter or margarine and perhaps a dusting with flour: the flour browns to give the cake a light crust. But tins for large cakes must be lined with paper to help the cooked cake slip out without breaking.

For a shallow tin, whether round or rectangular, a base lining will be enough. To help turn out a deep cake, the sides of the tin should be lined as well. For a long-cooking cake, such as a fruit cake, a double lining on the deep, round tin will prevent scorching.

Baking paper with a silicone coating is the best material for lining cake tins. In place of baking paper, you can also use well-greased greaseproof paper. Baking paper does not usually need greasing, though a light coating of butter is recommended in a few recipes, for stubborn mixtures that are particularly liable to stick.

Blind baking

Some pastry recipes in this book call for 'blind baking'. This is a process of pre-baking the pastry case before it has been filled. It's a necessary step when the filling isn't going to be baked, or when the filling takes less time to bake than the pastry. Blind baking lends other useful effects, such as preventing the crust from becoming soggy later, and helping to form a nice firm case for the filling.

Instructions for blind baking are generally given in the relevant recipes. Recipes may advise the use of baking beans or uncooked rice; use what you prefer. If you wish to know more about blind baking, consult a specialist pastry cookbook, or that wonderful treasure-trove of cooking advice – the internet.

Razzle-dazzle presentation

A piping bag is a great asset to a busy cook: it will turn a mere two tablespoons of whipped cream into a scrolled border or a cluster of rosettes. Chocolate curls account for far less effort (and calories) than a thick chocolate icing, yet look twice as professional.

An invaluable base or topping is meringue, made by whisking sugar into stiffly beaten egg whites. Cocoa, nuts or fruit purée can be added to meringue. It can be piped into intricate forms or incorporated into a layered assembly.

Happy baking adventures!

We hope this book provides you with all the recipes you need for your cake-worthy occasions, from everyday get-togethers to special celebrations. This book is designed to be friendly, easy to follow and, most importantly, oh-so-satisfying in terms of the results in your oven. Consider it your kitchen companion as you embark on these soft, crumbly, delicious adventures.

Good luck—and good baking.

Nanna's CLASSICS

Just like grandma used to make it

SANDWICH CAKE

4 eggs
¾ cup superfine (caster) sugar
1 cup self-rising (self-raising) flour
1 tablespoon cornstarch (cornflour)
1½ teaspoons melted butter
1 tablespoon confectioner's (icing) sugar, sifted

Jelly (jam) and cream filling
½ cup strawberry jelly (jam)
½ cup heavy (double) cream, whipped

1 Preheat oven to 360°F (180°C).

2 Place eggs in a bowl and beat until thick and creamy. Gradually beat in superfine sugar and continue beating until mixture becomes thick. This will take about 10 minutes.

3 Sift flour and cornstarch together over egg mixture, then fold in. Stir in ⅓ cup warm water and the melted butter.

4 Divide mixture evenly between two buttered and lined 8 in (20cm) round sandwich tins.

5 Bake for 20–25 minutes or until cakes shrink slightly from sides of tins and spring back when touched with the fingertips. Stand cakes in tins for 5 minutes before turning onto wire racks to cool.

6 To assemble, spread one cake with jelly, then top with whipped cream and remaining sponge cake. Just prior to serving, dust cake with confectioner's sugar.

Makes 1 cake • Preparation 30 minutes • Cooking 25 minutes

CHOCOLATE POUND CAKE

6 oz (185g) butter, softened
1¼ cups superfine (caster) sugar
3 teaspoons vanilla extract
3 eggs, lightly beaten
1½ cups self-rising (self-raising) flour
½ cup all-purpose (plain) flour
½ cup cocoa powder
1¼ cups milk
confectioner's (icing) sugar, for dusting

1 Preheat oven to 375°F (190°C). Place butter, sugar and vanilla in a bowl and beat until light and fluffy. Gradually beat in eggs.

2 Sift together self-rising flour, flour and cocoa powder. Fold flour mixture and milk alternately into butter mixture.

3 Pour mixture into a buttered and lined 8 in (20cm) square cake tin and bake for 55 minutes, or until cooked when tested with a skewer. Stand in tin for 10 minutes before turning onto a wire rack to cool. Serve with chocolate sauce and cream. Dust with confectioner's sugar.

Serves 8 • Preparation 30 minutes • Cooking 1 hour 5 minutes

GRANDMA'S CAKE

4 oz (125g) butter, softened
2 cups superfine (caster) sugar
2 eggs
2 teaspoons vanilla extract
1 cup self-rising (self-raising) flour
¾ cup all-purpose (plain) flour
¾ cup cocoa powder
1 cup buttermilk
¾ cup raspberry jelly (jam)

Chocolate sour cream filling
6 oz (185g) semisweet (dark)
  chocolate, broken into pieces
4 oz (125g) butter, chopped
3¼ cups confectioner's (icing) sugar,
  sifted
½ cup sour cream

1 Preheat oven to 360°F (180°C). Place butter, superfine sugar, eggs and
   vanilla in a bowl and beat until light and fluffy. Sift together self-rising flour,
   flour and cocoa powder.

2 Fold flour mixture and buttermilk alternately into butter mixture. Divide
   mixture between four buttered and lined 9 in (23cm) round cake tins and
   bake for 25 minutes or until cooked when tested with a skewer. Turn onto
   wire racks to cool.

3 To make filling, place chocolate and butter in a heatproof bowl set over a
   saucepan of simmering water and heat, stirring, until mixture is smooth.
   Remove bowl from pan. Add confectioner's sugar and sour cream and mix
   until smooth.

4 To assemble cake, place one cake on a serving plate, spread with some
   jelly and top with some filling. Top with a second cake, some more jelly and
   filling. Repeat layers until all cakes and jelly are used. Finish with a layer of
   cake and spread remaining filling over top and sides of cake.

Serves 8 • Preparation 30 minutes • Cooking 30 minutes

BAKED FUDGE WITH RUM SAUCE

2¼ cups sugar
⅔ cup all-purpose (plain) flour
⅔ cup cocoa powder
5 eggs, well beaten
7 oz (200g) butter
2 teaspoons vanilla extract
1 cup pecans, coarsely chopped

Sauce
1 egg yolk
½ cup confectioner's (icing) sugar, sifted
3 tablespoons light rum
1 cup heavy (double) cream, whipped

1 Preheat oven to 360°F (180°C). Mix sugar, flour and cocoa. Add to beaten eggs and blend thoroughly. Melt butter and add vanilla. Thoroughly combine butter and cocoa mixtures. Add nuts.

2 Bake in individual custard cups in a pan of hot water for 45 minutes to 1 hour. The fudge should be firm, like custard.

3 For sauce, mix together egg yolk, sugar and rum. Fold this mixture into stiffly whipped cream. Serve on top of the slightly warm baked fudge.

Serves 8 • Preparation 25 minutes • Cooking 60 minutes

DUTCH SPICE CAKE

4 oz (125g) butter
1½ cups brown sugar
4 eggs, beaten
½ cup milk
2½ cups all-purpose (plain) flour
1 teaspoon salt
1½ teaspoons baking powder
2 teaspoons ground cinnamon
¼ teaspoon ground cloves
¼ teaspoon ground nutmeg

1 Preheat oven to 360°F (180°C).

2 Place butter and sugar in a bowl and beat until light and fluffy. Add eggs and milk and beat well.

3 Sift flour, salt, baking powder, cinnamon, cloves and nutmeg together into butter mixture and mix well.

4 Spoon batter into a buttered and lined 8 in (20cm) round cake tin and bake for 1 hour or until cooked when tested with skewer. Stand in tin for 5 minutes before turning onto a wire rack to cool.

Makes 1 cake • Preparation 15 minutes • Cooking 1 hour

BUTTER CAKE

7 oz (200g) butter or margarine
1 teaspoon vanilla extract
1 cup superfine (caster) sugar
3 eggs
3 cups self-rising (self-raising) flour
pinch of salt
¾ cup milk

1 Preheat oven to 360°F (180°C).

2 In a large bowl, beat butter and vanilla extract together until softened. Add sugar gradually, beating until mixture is light and fluffy.

3 Lightly beat eggs and add gradually to the creamed mixture, beating well after each addition. If using an electric beater, add 1 tablespoon milk while beating the butter and sugar – this will help dissolve the sugar crystals.

4 Sift flour and salt. Using a large metal spoon, fold flour lightly into creamed mixture alternately with milk until mixture is smooth. Spoon mixture into a buttered 9 in (23cm) deep ring or kugelhpf tin. Bake for 40–45 minutes or until golden brown. Turn out onto a wire rack to cool.

Makes 1 cake • Preparation 15 minutes • Cooking 45 minutes

RECESS CAKE

2 eggs, separated
½ cup superfine (caster) sugar
¾ cup self-rising (self-raising) flour
pinch of salt
1 teaspoon butter or margarine, melted
¾ cup heavy (double) cream, whipped
8 oz (250g) strawberries, hulled

1 Preheat oven to 360°F (180°C).
2 Butter an 8 in (20cm) recess tin and dust lightly with cornstarch, shaking off any excess.
3 Beat egg whites until stiff peaks form, add sugar gradually and beat until thick and shiny.
4 Add egg yolks, one at a time, beating well after each addition.
5 Sift flour and salt together three times then fold lightly through the egg mixture.
6 Mix butter and 2 tablespoons boiling water together. Pour around the edge of the mixture and, using a metal spoon, gently fold in.
7 Pour the mixture into the prepared tin. Bake for 20–25 minutes or until sponge is firm to the touch.
8 Remove from the oven and sit on a wet kitchen towel for about 2 minutes (this helps to release the sponge without damage), then turn out onto a wire rack to cool. Fill the sponge with whipped cream and top with strawberries.

Makes 1 cake • Preparation 20 minutes • Cooking 30 minutes

NEW STYLE FRUIT CAKE

¾ cup all-purpose (plain) flour
½ cup baking powder
¾ cup superfine (caster) sugar
1½ cups Brazil nuts
1 cup glacé pineapple, chopped
1½ cups pitted dates, chopped
¾ cup candied peel
½ cup red glacé cherries
½ cup green glacé cherries
½ cup raisins
3 eggs, lightly beaten
1 teaspoon vanilla extract

1 Preheat oven to 280°F (140°C).

2 Sift together the flour, baking powder and sugar. Mix nuts and fruit in a large bowl and stir in sifted dry ingredients, eggs and vanilla. Spoon mixture into a lined and buttered 8 x 4 in (20 x 10 in) loaf tin and flatten with the back of a wooden spoon.

3 Bake in the lower half of the oven for 2–2½ hours. Allow to cool slightly in tin. Loosen edges and turn cake onto a cake cooler. Remove paper. When cold, wrap and store in refrigerator.

Makes 1 cake • Preparation 10 minutes • Cooking 2½ minutes

CLASSIC SAVARIN

2 tablespoons compressed yeast
1/3 cup warm milk
1 cup all-purpose (plain) flour, sifted
pinch of salt
2 teaspoons sugar
2 oz (60g) butter, softened
2 eggs

Syrup
1/4 cup sugar
2 tablespoons rum

1 Place yeast and warm milk in a small bowl, mix until yeast is dissolved.

2 Place flour in a bowl, make a well in the centre and pour in the yeast mixture. Add the salt, sugar and butter and stir until well combined. Add eggs one at a time, beating well after each addition. Continue beating until the dough is smooth. Cover bowl with a damp cloth and leave to rise in a warm place for 1 hour or until dough has doubled in size.

3 Knock the dough down by punching with your fist in the centre of mixture. Knead the mixture until smooth. Place dough into a greased 8 in (20cm) deep ring tin. Cover with greased cling wrap and leave in a warm place until dough has doubled in size.

4 Preheat oven to 450°F (230°C).

5 Remove cling wrap and bake in oven for 25 minutes or until firm to touch. If it starts to brown too quickly, cover with a piece of baking paper. Turn out onto a wire rack to cool.

6 To make the syrup, place sugar and 3/4 cup water into a heavy-based saucepan, cook over a low heat, stirring, until sugar dissolves. Bring to the boil and cook without stirring for 2 minutes. Remove from heat, add rum and mix well. Place savarin on a serving dish and spoon over hot syrup.

Makes 1 cake • Preparation 35 minutes • Cooking 25 minutes

CHERRY BUTTER CAKE

8 oz (250g) butter, softened
2 cups flour, sifted
4 eggs, separated
1 cup superfine (caster) sugar
2/3 cup glacé cherries
2 tablespoons flour, sifted with 1 teaspoon baking powder
glacé icing (page 385)
maraschino cherries

1 Preheat oven to 325°F (160°C).
2 Cream the butter, add the flour and beat until smooth and white.
3 Beat the egg whites until stiff, add egg yolks and sugar and continue beating until thick and frothy. Gradually add to the butter and flour mixture.
4 Stir in the cherries and the extra flour mixture. Pour into a buttered 8 in (20cm) tin or 6-cup cake mould and bake in the centre of the oven for 1¼ hours. Allow to cool, top with glacé icing and decorate with maraschino cherries.

Makes 1 cake • Preparation 25 minutes • Cooking 1¼ hours

PINEAPPLE FRUIT CAKE

16 oz (450g) canned crushed pineapple, undrained
1 cup superfine (caster) sugar
4 oz (125g) butter
2⅔ cups mixed fruit
pinch of salt
1 teaspoon mixed spice
1 teaspoon baking soda (bicarbonate of soda)
2 eggs, lightly beaten
1 cup flour, sifted with 1 cup self-rising (self-raising) flour

1 Preheat oven to 320°F (160°C).

2 Bring the combined pineapple, sugar, butter, mixed fruit, salt and mixed spice to the boil over high heat and cook for 15 minutes. Add baking soda and allow to cool. Add the eggs and sifted flour and beat thoroughly. Pour into an 8 in (20cm) cake tin lined with 2 layers each of brown and baking paper.

3 Bake in the lower half of the oven for 2–2½ hours. Allow to cool slightly before removing from tin.

Makes 1 cake • Preparation 10 minutes • Cooking 2 hours 30 minutes

BANANA CAKE WITH MAPLE ICING

2 cups self-rising (self-raising) flour
4 oz (125g) butter or margarine
¾ cup superfine (caster) sugar
½ teaspoon vanilla extract
3 medium, very ripe bananas, peeled and roughly mashed
2 eggs
½ cup natural yogurt

Frosting
1½ oz (45g) butter or margarine
¾ cup confectioner's (icing) sugar, sifted
2 teaspoons maple syrup
sliced banana, extra

1 Preheat oven to 360°F (180°C).

2 Butter an 8 x 6 in (20 x 15cm) loaf tin with melted butter or margarine and line the base with buttered baking paper. Sift the flour into a mixing bowl. Beat the butter or margarine until soft, add the sugar, vanilla and bananas and continue beating until the mixture is light and fluffy. Add 2 tablespoons of the flour and beat until well combined. Add the eggs one at a time, beating well after each addition.

3 Gently fold the remaining flour into the creamed mixture alternately with the yogurt. Spoon mixture into the prepared tin and smooth the top level.

4 Bake for 1 hour or until golden brown and firm. Cool in the tin for 5 minutes, then turn out onto a wire rack and allow to cool completely.

5 For the frosting, beat butter or margarine in a small bowl until soft and creamy, add confectioner's sugar and maple syrup and continue beating until mixture is smooth. Spread over cooled cake, decorate with sliced banana.

Makes 1 cake • Preparation 35 minutes • Cooking 1 hour

FRUITY CARROT LOAF

1 cup whole wheat self-rising (wholemeal self-raising) flour
½ cup rye flour
½ cup raw sugar
½ teaspoon salt
½ tablespoon baking soda (bicarbonate of soda)
1 teaspoon ground cinnamon
½ cup crushed pineapple, undrained
1 cup grated carrot
2 eggs
½ cup oil
1 teaspoon vanilla extract
½ cup chopped walnuts
lemon glacé icing (page 385)

1 Preheat oven to 360°F (180°C).

2 Butter an 8 x 6 in (20 x 15cm) loaf tin with melted butter or margarine and line the base with buttered baking paper. Sift the flours, sugar, salt, baking soda and cinnamon into a mixing bowl. Add the crushed pineapple, carrot, eggs, oil and vanilla and beat until well combined. Stir the chopped walnuts into the carrot mixture. Spoon the batter into prepared loaf tin. Bake for 25–30 minutes or until a skewer inserted in the centre comes out clean.

3 Remove from the oven and allow to cool in the tin for 5 minutes before turning out onto a wire rack to cool completely.

4 Top loaf with lemon glacé icing (page 385).

Makes 1 loaf • Preparation 30 minutes • Cooking 30 minutes

CARROT AND WALNUT CAKE

1¾ cups self-rising (self-raising) flour
⅔ cup whole wheat self-rising (wholemeal self-raising) flour
½ teaspoon baking soda (bicarbonate of soda)
2 teaspoons mixed spice
½ teaspoon ground nutmeg
½ cup raisins
½ cup chopped walnuts
½ cup brown sugar
¼ cup olive oil
2 eggs
⅔ cup buttermilk
2 teaspoons vanilla extract
1½ cups grated carrot
8 oz (250g) canned crushed pineapple in natural juice, undrained
cream cheese frosting (page 385)

1 Preheat oven to 360°F (180°C).

2 Sift flours, baking soda, mixed spice and nutmeg into a bowl. Add raisins and walnuts.

3 In a separate bowl, beat sugar and oil until light and fluffy. Beat in eggs one at a time. Stir in buttermilk and vanilla extract.

4 Fold in flour mixture, carrot and pineapple and pour mixture into a buttered and lined 9 in (23cm) round cake tin.

5 Bake for 20–25 minutes or until cooked when tested with a skewer.

6 Stand for about 5 minutes and then turn onto a wire rack to cool.

7 Spread cold cake with cream cheese frosting (page 385).

Makes 1 cake • Preparation 30 minutes • Cooking 25 minutes

ALMOND AND APRICOT LOAF

4 oz (125g) dried apricots, chopped
2 oz (60g) butter
¾ cup sugar
1 egg, lightly beaten
1 cup whole wheat (wholemeal) flour
1 cup all-purpose (plain) flour
1 teaspoon baking soda (bicarbonate of soda)
½ cup almonds, chopped

1 Preheat oven to 360°F (180°C).
2 Combine apricots, butter, sugar and 1 cup boiling water in a bowl, stir until butter melts and sugar dissolves, cool to room temperature.
3 Stir in egg, then stir in sifted flours and baking soda in two lots. Stir in almonds.
4 Spread mixture into a buttered and lined 8 x 6 in (20 x 15cm) loaf tin. Bake for 1 hour or until golden brown and cooked through.

Serves 6 • Preparation 25 minutes • Cooking 1 hour

SPICED APPLE WHOLEMEAL CAKE

2 apples, peeled, cored and sliced
4 oz (125g) butter
1 cup raw sugar
2 eggs
1 cup whole wheat all-purpose (wholemeal plain) flour
1 cup self-rising (self-raising) flour
½ teaspoon baking powder
1 teaspoon mixed spice
¼ cup walnuts
½ cup raisins, chopped
¾ cup heavy (whipping) cream
sifted confectioner's (icing) sugar for decoration

1 Preheat oven to 360°F (180°C). Butter and line a 9 in (23cm) round cake tin.
2 Cook apples in ¾ cup water until tender. Remove from heat, purée and sieve until smooth, then cool.
3 Cream butter and sugar in a small bowl until light and fluffy. Add eggs, beat until combined.
4 Sift the flour, baking powder and mixed spice together. Add half the sifted dry ingredients and half the apple mixture, beat until combined. Add remaining dry ingredients and apple mixture, beat until combined. Stir in walnuts and raisins.
5 Spread mixture evenly into prepared tin. Bake for 40 minutes or until golden brown. Turn onto wire rack to cool. When cold, split cake in half, fill with whipped cream and dust with confectioner's sugar.

Makes 1 cake • Preparation 40 minutes • Cooking 40 minutes

PUMPKIN NUT SLICE

6 oz (170g) butter or margarine
1 cup superfine (caster) sugar
1 cup all-purpose (plain) flour
1 teaspoon baking soda (bicarbonate
  of soda)
½ teaspoon baking powder
½ teaspoon salt
1½ teaspoons ground cinnamon
½ teaspoon allspice
2 eggs, lightly beaten
½ cup chopped pecans or walnuts
½ teaspoon vanilla extract
½ cup chopped raisins

1 cup drained, crushed pineapple
¾ cup cooked, mashed pumpkin

Frosting
1½ cups sifted confectioner's (icing)
  sugar
8 oz (250g) cream cheese, softened
½ teaspoon vanilla extract
2 teaspoons lemon juice

1 Preheat oven to 360°F (180°C).

2 Butter and line the base of a 9 x 9 in (23 x 23cm) square tin. Beat the butter
   or margarine until soft. Add sugar and beat until mixture is light and fluffy.

3 Sift all dry ingredients together and add to the creamed mixture alternately
   with the beaten eggs. Stir in the nuts, vanilla extract, raisins, pineapple and
   pumpkin. Mix well and pour into the tin.

4 Bake for 1 hour or until skewer inserted in the centre of the cake comes out
   clean. Cool on a wire rack.

5 To make the frosting, place all the ingredients in a mixing bowl and beat
   until well combined, then increase speed and beat until light and fluffy.
   Spread frosting over cake.

Serves 6–8 • Preparation 40 minutes • Cooking 1 hour

RHUBARB SOUFFLE

1 lb (500g) rhubarb, trimmed and cut into 1 in (2½cm) pieces
½ cup sugar
4 teaspoons cornstarch (cornflour), blended with ¼ cup water
½ cup superfine (caster) sugar
5 egg whites
confectioner's (icing) sugar, sifted

1 Preheat ovent to 430°F (220°C).
2 Place rhubarb, ½ cup water and the sugar in a saucepan and cook over a medium heat for 10 minutes or until rhubarb softens.
3 Stir in cornstarch mixture and cook for 2–3 minutes longer or until mixture thickens. Set aside to cool slightly.
4 Place egg whites in a large mixing bowl and beat until soft peaks form. Gradually add superfine sugar, beating well after each addition, until mixture is thick and glossy.
5 Fold in rhubarb mixture and spoon into a buttered 8 in (20cm) soufflé dish, or suitable individual soufflé dishes. Bake for 15–20 minutes or until soufflé is well risen and golden brown. Dust with confectioner's sugar and serve immediately.

Serves 8 • Preparation 20 minutes • Cooking 40 minutes

BRANDIED PLUM CLAFOUTI

1 lb (500g) plums, quartered and stoned
1/3 cup brandy
2 tablespoons sugar
1/4 cup all-purpose (plain) flour, sifted
1/4 cup superfine (caster) sugar
3 eggs, lightly beaten
1 cup milk
1 teaspoon vanilla extract

Brandy orange sauce
3/4 cup orange juice
2 tablespoons sugar
1/2 teaspoon ground cinnamon
2 teaspoons arrowroot, blended with 4 teaspoons water

1 Preheat oven to 360°F (180°C).
2 Place plums and brandy in a bowl, sprinkle with sugar, cover and set aside to stand for 30 minutes. Drain plums and reserve liquid. Arrange plums in a lightly buttered ovenproof dish.
3 Place flour and superfine sugar in a bowl, add eggs, milk and vanilla extract and stir until batter is smooth. Pour batter evenly over plums. Bake for 45–50 minutes or until firm.
4 To make sauce, place reserved brandy liquid, orange juice, sugar, cinnamon and arrowroot mixture in a small saucepan and cook over a medium heat, stirring constantly, until mixture boils and thickens. Accompany clafouti with brandy orange sauce and whipped cream, if desired.

Serves 4 • Preparation 50 minutes • Cooking 50 minutes

SPICED APPLE CAKE

2 apples, cored, peeled and sliced
4 oz (125g) butter
1 cup raw sugar
2 eggs
1 cup self-rising (self-raising) flour
1 cup whole wheat (wholemeal) flour
½ teaspoon baking soda (bicarbonate of soda)
1½ teaspoons ground mixed spice
2 tablespoons walnuts, chopped
⅓ cup raisins, chopped
¾ cup heavy (double) cream, whipped
confectioner's (icing) sugar, sifted

1 Preheat oven to 360°F (180°C).

2 Place apples and ¾ cup water in a saucepan and cook over a medium heat until tender. Place in a food processor or blender and process until smooth. Set aside to cool.

3 Place butter and sugar in a bowl and beat until light and fluffy. Add eggs, one at a time, beating well after each addition.

4 Sift together self-rising flour, whole wheat flour, baking soda and 1 teaspoon of the mixed spice into a bowl. Return husks to bowl. Mix flour mixture and apple mixture, alternately, into butter mixture, then stir in walnuts and raisins.

5 Spoon batter into a buttered and lined 9 in (23cm) round cake tin and bake for 40 minutes or until cooked when tested with a skewer. Allow to cool in tin for 5 minutes before turning onto a wire rack to cool completely.

6 Split cake in half horizontally, spread bottom half with cream, then top with other half and dust with remaining mixed spice and confectioner's sugar.

Makes 1 cake • Preparation 20 minutes • Cooking 50 minutes

ESPRESSO CAKE

½ cup finely ground espresso coffee beans
6 oz (200g) butter
1¼ cups sugar
3 eggs
1 tablespoon vanilla extract
2 cups all-purpose (plain) flour
3 teaspoons baking powder

Coffee cream
1¼ cup heavy (double) cream
1 tablespoon confectioner's (icing) sugar
2 tablespoons very strong espresso coffee

1 Preheat oven to 360°F (180°C).

2 Pour 1 cup boiling water over half the ground coffee beans and leave to steep for 5 minutes. Strain liquid from beans and pour over butter in a large bowl, stirring until butter melts. Discard the strained beans.

3 Mix in sugar, eggs and vanilla and beat with a wooden spoon until combined. Sift flour and baking powder into mixture and mix in with remaining ground coffee beans.

4 Pour the mixture into a lined 8 in (20cm) square cake tin. Bake for 50–55 minutes or until cake springs back when lightly touched.

5 Cool in tin for 10 minutes before turning onto a cooling rack. Dust with cinnamon and serve with coffee cream.

6 To make the coffee cream, whip cream until soft, then beat in confectioner's sugar and coffee.

Serves 8–10 • Preparation 30 minutes • Cooking 60 minutes

COFFEE SANDWICH CAKE

9 oz (250g) butter, room temperature
1 cup superfine (caster) sugar
6 eggs, lightly beaten
2 cups self-rising (self-raising) flour

Frosting
2 oz (60g) butter, softened
¾ cup confectioner's (icing) sugar
½ teaspoon ground cinnamon

2 teaspoons instant coffee powder,
   dissolved in 2 teaspoons hot water,
   then cooled

Filling
1 tablespoon coffee liqueur
½ cup heavy (double) cream, whipped

1 Preheat oven to 320°F (160°C).
2 Place butter and sugar in a food processor and process until creamy. Add eggs and sifted flour and process until all ingredients are combined.
3 Spoon batter into two buttered and lined 7 in (18cm) sandwich tins and bake for 30–35 minutes or until golden and cooked when tested with a skewer. Turn cakes onto wire racks to cool.
4 To make frosting, place butter, sifted confectioner's sugar, cinnamon and coffee mixture in a food processor and process until light and fluffy.
5 To make filling, fold liqueur into whipped cream.
6 Spread filling over one cake and top with remaining cake. Spread frosting over top of cake.

Serves 6–8 • Preparation 60 minutes • Cooking 35 minutes

PANETTONE

1 tablespoon dried yeast
½ cup sugar
1⅓ cup fine flour
2 eggs separated
½ teaspoon salt
2 oz (60g) softened butter
2 teaspoons vanilla essence
⅔ cup raisins
4 tablespoons mixed peel

1 Grease a deep tin with margarine. Dissolve yeast in ½ cup of warm water with 1 tablespoon of the sugar and half the flour. Mix well, cover and allow to rise until puffy – about 20 minutes.

2 Beat egg whites, salt and remaining sugar until stiff, and add to the dough, alternating with remainder of the flour.

3 Add egg yolks and softened butter then beat with electric mixer for 2 minutes. Cover and let mixture rise again until doubled, about 20 minutes. Punch down and add the vanilla essence.

4 Preheat the oven to 320°F (160°C). Pour a little mixture into tin, add raisins and peel, then more mixture, continuing this method until all the fruit and mixture is used. Allow mixture to stand for about 30 minutes or until the tin is three-parts full. Cook for 40 minutes on low shelf.

Serves 2–4 • Preparation 1 hour 15 minutes • Cooking 40 minutes

YELLOW PEACH STRUDEL

4 large yellow peaches, peeled and sliced
¾ cup sugar
1 tablespoon gelatin
3½ oz (100g) butter
1 egg
2 cups all-purpose (plain) flour
2 tablespoons pure confectioner's (icing) sugar

1 Preheat the oven to 360°F (180°C). Soak the gelatin in ¼ cup cold water, then heat gently until dissolved. Cool. Combine all the pastry ingredients with the gelatin mixture in a food processor and process to form a firm pastry.

2 Divide the pastry and press half the mixture into a shallow 8 in (20cm) square ungreased cake pan with your fingers. Place the peeled and sliced peaches on the pastry base, then sprinkle with ½ cup sugar.

3 Roll out the other half of the pastry for the top of the strudel. Cut pastry into strips and use to form a lattice over the fresh peach slices.

4 Glaze with the reserved egg white and sprinkle with remaining sugar. Place in the oven and bake for 35 minutes. Serve with cream.

Serves 4 • Preparation 40 minutes • Cooking 35 minutes

Decadent
CHOCOLATE

Say it with cocoa

CHOCOLATE HAZELNUT TORTE

9 oz (250g) semisweet (dark) chocolate, broken into pieces
6 eggs, separated
1 cup sugar
2 cups hazelnuts, toasted and roughly chopped (see note)
1 tablespoon rum
confectioner's (icing) sugar, for dusting

1 Preheat the oven to 375°F (190°C). Place chocolate in a heatproof bowl set over a saucepan of simmering water and heat, stirring, until chocolate melts. Remove bowl from pan and cool slightly.

2 Place egg yolks and sugar in a bowl and beat until thick and pale. Fold chocolate, hazelnuts and rum into egg mixture.

3 Place egg whites into a clean bowl and beat until stiff peaks form. Fold egg whites into chocolate mixture. Pour mixture into a buttered and lined 9 in (23cm) springform tin and bake for 50 minutes or until cooked when tested with a skewer. Cool cake in tin. Just prior to serving, dust cake with confectioner's sugar.

Note: To toast hazelnuts, place nuts on a baking tray and bake for 10 minutes or until skins begin to split. Place on a tea towel and rub to remove skins. Place in a food processor and process to roughly chop.

Serves 8 • Preparation 40 minutes • Cooking 50 minutes

MISSISSIPPI MUD CAKE

9 oz (250g) butter, chopped coarsely
7 oz (200g) semisweet (dark) eating chocolate, chopped coarsely
1⅓ cups milk
2 cups superfine (caster) sugar
1 teaspoon vanilla extract
1½ cups all-purpose (plain) flour
¼ cup self-rising (self-raising) flour
¼ cup cocoa
2 eggs

Chocolate ganache
⅓ cup cream
7 oz (200g) semisweet (dark) eating chocolate, chopped coarsely

1 Preheat oven to 340°F (170°C). Grease a deep 8½ in (22cm) round cake pan and line the base with baking paper.

2 Combine butter, chocolate, milk, sugar and extract in a medium saucepan. Stir over low heat until mixture is smooth.

3 Cool mixture until barely warm, then whisk in the sifted dry ingredients and eggs. Pour mixture into pan, and bake about 1½ hours. Stand cake for 5 minutes before turning onto wire rack to cool.

4 To make chocolate ganache, bring cream to the boil in small saucepan. Remove from heat and add chocolate, stirring until smooth, then pour over the cake. You could also refrigerate the ganache for about 30 minutes, beat with a wooden spoon or electric mixer until smooth, then spread over cake.

Serves 12 • Preparation 30-45 minutes • Cooking 1 hour 30 minutes

CHOCOLATE SUNDAE

6 scoops of your favourite
  ice cream

Brownie base
9 oz (250g) butter, melted
4 eggs, lightly beaten
1¼ cups superfine (caster) sugar
2 teaspoons vanilla extract
¾ cup all-purpose (plain) flour, sifted

¼ cup cocoa powder, sifted
1½ oz (45g) pecans, chopped

Fudge sauce
2 cups brown sugar
¼ cup cocoa powder, sifted
1 cup heavy (double) cream
1 oz (30g) butter

1 Preheat oven to 360°F (180°C). To make base, place butter, eggs, superfine
   sugar and vanilla in a bowl and beat to combine. Add flour, cocoa powder,
   and pecans and mix well to combine.

2 Pour mixture into a buttered and lined 7¾ in (20cm) square cake tin and
   bake for 30 minutes or until firm to touch, but still fudgy in the centre. Cool
   in tin, then cut into six squares.

3 To make sauce, place brown sugar, cocoa powder, cream and butter in a
   saucepan and cook over a low heat, stirring constantly, until sugar dissolves.
   Bring to the boil, then reduce heat and simmer for 5 minutes or until sauce
   thickens slightly.

4 To assemble sundaes, top each brownie square with a scoop of ice cream.
   Drizzle with hot sauce and serve.

Serves 6 • Preparation 10 minutes • Cooking 40 minutes

MASCARPONE ROULADE

6 oz (185g) semisweet (dark) chocolate
¼ cup strong black coffee
5 eggs, separated
½ cup superfine (caster) sugar
2 tablespoons self-rising (self-raising)
   flour, sifted
½ cup chocolate hazelnut spread
frosted rose petals (see note)

Mascarpone filling
13 oz (375g) mascarpone
2 tablespoons confectioner's (icing)
   sugar, sifted
2 tablespoons brandy

1 Preheat oven to 320°F (160°C). Place chocolate and coffee in a heatproof
   bowl set over a saucepan of simmering water and heat, stirring, until
   smooth. Cool slightly.
2 Beat egg yolks until thick and pale. Gradually beat in superfine sugar. Fold
   chocolate mixture and flour into egg yolks.
3 Beat egg whites until stiff peaks form. Fold into chocolate mixture. Pour
   mixture into a buttered and lined 10 x 1 in (26 x 3cm) Swiss roll tin and bake
   for 20 minutes or until firm. Cool in tin.
4 To make filling, beat mascarpone, confectioner's sugar and brandy in a bowl.
5 Turn cakes onto a clean tea towel sprinkled with superfine sugar. Spread
   with chocolate hazelnut spread and half the filling, and roll up. Spread with
   remaining filling and decorate with frosted rose petals.

**Note: To make frosted rose petals, lightly whisk egg white in a shallow bowl and dip
in fresh, dry petals to lightly cover. Dip petals in superfine sugar, shake off excess
and stand on baking paper to harden.**

Serves 8–10 • Preparation 30 minutes • Cooking 30 minutes

CASSATA LAYERS

8 in (20cm) sponge cake (page 125)
¼ cup almond liqueur
chocolate curls (page 392)

Cassata filling
36 oz (1L) vanilla ice cream, softened (see note)
1 cup heavy (double) cream
4 oz (125g) glacé apricots, chopped
4 oz (125g) glacé pineapple, chopped
2 oz (60g) glacé cherries, chopped
2 oz (60g) raisins, halved
4 oz (125g) semisweet (dark) chocolate, grated
4 oz (125g) pistachios, chopped

1 To make the sponge, see Simple Sponge Cake recipe, page 125.
2 To make filling, place ice cream, cream, apricots, pineapple, cherries, raisins, chocolate and pistachios in a bowl and mix to combine.
3 Split sponge horizontally into three even layers. Place one layer of sponge in the base of a lined 8 in (20cm) springform tin and sprinkle with 1 tablespoon of liqueur. Top with one-third of the filling. Repeat layers to use all ingredients, ending with filling layer. Freeze for 5 hours or until firm. Remove from freezer 1 hour before serving and place in refrigerator.
4 Just prior to serving, decorate with chocolate curls (page 392).

Note: Use the best quality ice cream available. To retain maximum volume and creamy texture, keep the cassata filling mixture well chilled until the cassata is finally assembled.

Serves 10 • Preparation and cooking 5 hours 50 minutes

FROZEN MAPLE NUT PARFAIT

6 egg yolks
1 cup superfine (caster) sugar
½ cup maple syrup
2½ cups heavy (double) cream
3½ oz (100g) macadamias, finely chopped
3½ oz (100g) white chocolate, chopped

1. Place egg yolks in a bowl and beat until thick and pale. Place sugar and ½ cup water in a saucepan and heat over a low heat, stirring, until sugar dissolves. Bring to the boil and boil until mixture thickens and reaches soft ball stage or 245°F (118°C) on a sugar thermometer.

2. Gradually beat sugar mixture and maple syrup into egg yolks and continue beating until mixture cools. Place cream in a bowl and beat until soft peaks form. Fold cream, macadamias and chocolate into egg mixture.

3. Pour mixture into an aluminium foil-lined 6 x 9¾ in (15 x 25cm) loaf tin and freeze for 5 hours or until firm.

4. Turn parfait onto a serving plate, remove foil, cut into slices and drizzle with extra maple syrup.

This light and luscious frozen Italian meringue is the perfect partner for a garnish of fresh fruit and perhaps some almond biscotti.

Serves 8 • Preparation 5 hours 40 minutes

CHRISTMAS PECAN PIE

2½ cups chocolate wafer crumbs
2 oz (60g) butter, melted, plus 3 oz (90g) softened
¾ cup brown sugar
3 eggs
1½ cups semisweet (dark) chocolate buttons, melted
2 teaspoons instant coffee
1 teaspoon vanilla extract
½ cup flour
1 cup pecans, coarsely chopped
½ cup whipping cream
morello cherries, optional

1 Preheat oven to 360°F (180°C). Combine chocolate wafer crumbs and $^1/_3$ cup melted butter; firmly press on bottom and sides of a 8½ in (22cm) tart pan or pie plate. Bake for 6–8 minutes.

2 Cream the softened butter. Gradually add brown sugar with the electric mixer at medium speed until blended. Add the eggs one at a time, beating after each addition. Stir in the melted chocolate, instant coffee, vanilla, flour and chopped pecans.

3 Pour into the prepared crust. Bake at 365°F (185°C) for 25 minutes. Remove from oven and cool completely on a rack.

4 Serve with whipped cream with morello cherries stirred through.

Serves 6 • Preparation 50 minutes • Cooking 35 minutes

JAFFA PECAN CAKES

3½ oz (100g) semisweet (dark) chocolate, chopped
4 oz (125g) butter
2 eggs, beaten
2 tablespoons orange liqueur
finely grated zest of ½ orange
¼ cup superfine (caster) sugar
4 tablespoons pecans, chopped
½ cup all-purpose (plain) flour, sifted
18 pecan halves

1 Preheat oven to 360°F (180°C).
2 Place chopped chocolate and butter in a heatproof bowl set over a saucepan of simmering water and cook, stirring, until chocolate and butter melt and mixture is combined. Remove bowl from heat and set aside to cool slightly.
3 Stir eggs, liqueur, orange zest, sugar and chopped pecans into chocolate mixture and mix to combine. Fold in flour.
4 Spoon batter into patty tins lined with paper cake cases, top each with a pecan half and bake for 20 minutes or until cakes are cooked when tested with a skewer. Remove cakes from patty tins and allow to cool on wire racks.

Makes 18 cakes • Preparation 25 minutes • Cooking 20 minutes

MUDDY MUD CAKE

8 oz (250g) butter, softened
8 oz (250g) bittersweet chocolate, chopped
½ cup superfine (caster) sugar
½ cup brown sugar
1½ tablespoons brandy
1⅓ cup all-purpose (plain) flour
1 teaspoon baking powder
3 tablespoons cocoa powder
2 eggs
1 teaspoon vanilla extract

Hot fudge sauce
1 cup white sugar
½ cup brown sugar
½ cup cocoa powder
2 tablespoons all-purpose (plain) flour
¼ teaspoon salt
1 oz (30g) butter
¼ teaspoon vanilla extract

1 Preheat the oven to 300°F (150°C) and butter a 9½ in (24cm) non-stick springform cake tin, or small moulds.

2 In a saucepan, melt the butter, then add the chocolate, sugars, brandy and 1½ cups water. Mix well with a whisk until the mixture is smooth.

3 Sift together the flour, baking powder and cocoa and add to the chocolate mixture with the eggs and vanilla. Beat until just combined – don't worry if the mixture is lumpy.

4 Pour into the cake tin and bake for 50 minutes or, if using moulds, 30 minutes. Allow to cool in the tin or moulds for 15 minutes, then turn out.

5 To make hot fudge sauce, mix dry ingredients in a medium saucepan and add butter and ¾ cup water. Bring to the boil and continue boiling for about 10 minutes. Remove from heat and add vanilla extract.

6 Dust with confectioner's sugar and serve warm with cream or ice cream and hot fudge sauce.

Serves 6 • Preparation 20 minutes • Cooking 50 minutes

CHOCOLATE FUDGE TORTE

3 oz (90g) butter
¾ cup superfine (caster) sugar
5 eggs, separated
2½ oz (75g) semisweet (dark) chocolate, melted
2 tablespoons brandy
3 oz (90g) ground almonds
½ cup fresh white breadcrumbs

Topping
4 oz (125g) dark Toblerone, melted
2 tablespoons dark corn syrup
½ oz (15g) butter, melted
1 tablespoon heavy (double) cream

1 Preheat oven to 360°F (180°C).
2 Beat butter and sugar together until pale and creamy. Beat in the egg yolks one at a time, then beat in melted chocolate and brandy. Fold in the ground almonds and breadcrumbs, mix well.
3 Beat egg whites until soft peaks form, fold into chocolate mixture in two batches. Pour into a baking paper-lined and flour dusted 9 in (23cm) springform tin. Bake for 30–35 minutes. Turn out onto a wire rack to cool.
4 To make the topping, combine Toblerone, corn syrup, butter and cream in a small saucepan over low heat, stir until combined. Spread over cooled cake.

Serves 8 • Preparation 20 minutes • Cooking 35 minutes

CHOCOLATE PECAN TORTE

4 egg whites
$^{1}/_{3}$ cup superfine (caster) sugar
2 tablespoons cocoa powder, sifted
1 cup chopped pecans, extra to decorate
5 oz (150g) semisweet (dark) chocolate, grated
1 cup heavy (double) cream, whipped

1 Preheat oven to 320°F (160°C).

2 Beat egg whites in a large bowl until soft peaks form. Gradually add sugar, beat for a further 5 minutes until mixture is thick and glossy.

3 Fold in cocoa, pecans and grated chocolate, spread mixture into a buttered and lined 9 in (23cm) springform tin.

4 Bake for 45 minutes. Leave to cool in tin. Decorate torte with whipped cream and extra pecan nuts.

Serves 6–8 • Preparation 20 minutes • Cooking 45 minutes

DARK CHOCOLATE CAKE

¾ cup cocoa powder
1¾ cups self-rising (self-raising) flour
1½ cups superfine (caster) sugar
6 eggs, separated
3 oz (90g) butter, melted

Filling

1¼ cups confectioner's (icing) sugar
¼ cup milk
1 tablespoon vanilla extract
2 tablespoons cocoa powder
8 oz (250g) cream cheese, softened

Decoration

1 cup chopped nuts
½ cup whole pecans
¼ cup heavy (double) cream
4 oz (125g) milk chocolate, melted

1 Preheat oven to 320°F (160°C).

2 Blend cocoa with ¾ cup boiling water until smooth. Place flour and sugar in a large bowl, beat in cocoa mixture, egg yolks and melted butter until mixture is smooth.

3 Beat egg whites in a separate bowl until soft peaks form, fold into chocolate mixture in two batches. Pour mixture into a buttered and lined 9 in (23cm) springform tin.

4 Bake for 1 hour or until cooked when tested. Turn onto a wire rack to cool. When cake is completely cold, cut into three layers.

5 To make the filling, mix together confectioner's sugar, milk, vanilla and cocoa, stir until smooth. Blend or process together with cream cheese until smooth. Spread two of the cake layers with the filling (reserve ½ cup of filling for side of cake) and sandwich cake together. Spread remaining filling over edge of cake. Chill for 1 hour to set filling.

6 Sprinkle nuts onto bench top, turn cake on its side and roll edge onto nuts, pressing gently until the cake is covered in nuts, all the way around.

7 Combine melted milk chocolate and cream in a small bowl, mix well. Spread top of cake with mixture, chill to set. Decorate cake with pecans.

Serves 6–8 • Preparation 1 hour 20 minutes • Cooking 1 hour

CRUSTED RUM FUDGE CAKE

4 oz (125g) butter
1 cup brown sugar
2 eggs, separated
1 cup chopped raisins
4 oz (125g) chocolate, melted
2½ cups self-rising (self-raising) flour
pinch of salt
½ teaspoon ground cinnamon
½ cup sour milk (see note)
1 tablespoon rum

1 Preheat oven to 360°F (180°C).

2 Cream the butter and sugar until light and fluffy. Add the egg yolks, raisins and chocolate and beat thoroughly. Sift the self-rising flour, salt and cinnamon.

3 Combine sour milk with rum and ¼ cup hot water. Fold both the flour and milk mixtures into the egg mixture alternately. Beat egg whites until stiff and fold through cake mixture. Pour into a lined and buttered 8 in (20cm) cake tin.

4 Bake in the centre of the oven for 1–1¼ hours. Allow to cool in tin. Dust with confectioner's sugar to serve.

Note: Fresh milk may be used instead of sour milk, or milk may be soured by the addition of ½ teaspoon lemon juice or vinegar.

Makes 1 cake • Preparation 25 minutes • Cooking 1¼ hours

STRAWBERRY CHOCOLATE CAKE

1 tablespoon vinegar
1 cup milk
1½ cups all-purpose (plain) flour
pinch of salt
½ cup cocoa powder
1½ teaspoons baking soda
   (bicarbonate of soda)
¼ cups superfine (caster) sugar
7 oz (200g) butter or margarine,
   melted and cooled
1 teaspoon vanilla extract
2 eggs, lightly beaten

Filling
1 cup heavy (double) cream, lightly
   whipped, extra to decorate
1 cup fanned strawberries (page 393)

1 Preheat oven to 360°F (180°C).

2 Add vinegar to milk, stir and set aside.

3 Sift flour, salt, cocoa, baking soda and sugar into a bowl. Pour in the melted butter and half the soured milk, and beat well for 2 minutes. Add vanilla extract, the remaining soured milk and eggs, and beat for another 2 minutes.

4 Pour mixture into two buttered 9 in (23cm) sandwich tins that have been base-lined with buttered baking paper. Bake for 30–35 minutes or until a skewer inserted in the centre comes out clean. Allow to cool in the tins for 5 minutes, then turn out onto a wire rack to cool.

5 When cold, spread one cake with whipped cream and arrange fanned strawberries (page 393) over the cream. Place the other cake on top. Spread cream over the top of cake and place fanned strawberry in the middle.

Makes 1 cake • Preparation 20 minutes • Cooking 35 minutes

CHOCOLATE LUA CAKE

3 whole eggs, plus 2 egg yolks
2/3 cup superfine (caster) sugar
1/3 cup all-purpose (plain) flour
1/3 cup cocoa powder
1/4 cup self-rising (self-raising) flour
2 oz (60g) butter, melted, combined with 2–3 tablespoons Kahlua or Tia Maria
1 1/4 cups whipping cream, whipped with 2 tablespoons Kahlua or Tia Maria
grated chocolate, to decorate

1 Preheat oven to 360°F (180°C).
2 Place eggs, egg yolks and sugar in a bowl. Whisk over hot water until thick and frothy. Remove from the water and whisk until cold. Sift together the all-purpose flour, cocoa and self-rising flour.
3 Gently fold into the egg mixture alternately with the butter mixture. Place into a buttered and lined 8 in (20cm) cake tin. Bake for 30–35 minutes. When cold, slice cake into three, sprinkle each layer with Kahlua or Tia Maria and fill with the cream.
4 Refrigerate overnight. Sprinkle top with grated chocolate before serving.

Makes 1 cake • Preparation 20 minutes • Cooking 35 minutes

RASPBERRY TRUFFLE CAKES

½ cup cocoa powder, sifted
4 oz (125g) butter
1¾ cups superfine (caster) sugar
2 eggs
1⅔ cups self-rising (self-raising) flour, sifted
14 oz (400g) semisweet (dark) chocolate, melted
fresh raspberries

Raspberry cream
4 oz (125g) raspberries, puréed and sieved
½ cup heavy (double) cream, whipped

1 Preheat oven to 360°F (180°C).
2 Combine cocoa powder and 1 cup boiling water. Mix to dissolve and set aside to cool.
3 Place butter and sugar in a bowl and beat until light and fluffy. Beat in eggs, one at a time, adding a little flour with each egg. Fold remaining flour and cocoa mixture, alternately, into creamed butter mixture.
4 Spoon mixture into eight lightly buttered ½-cup capacity ramekins or large muffin tins. Bake for 20–25 minutes or until cakes are cooked when tested with a skewer. Cool for 5 minutes, then turn onto wire racks to cool. Turn cakes upside down and scoop out centre, leaving a ½ in (12mm) shell. Spread each cake with chocolate to cover top and sides, then place right way up on a wire rack.
5 To make cream, fold raspberry purée into cream. Spoon cream into a piping bag fitted with a large nozzle. Carefully turn cakes upside down and pipe in cream to fill cavity. Place right way up on individual serving plates. Garnish with fresh raspberries.

Serves 8 • Preparation 25 minutes • Cooking 25 minutes

CHOC CHIP ORANGE CAKE

1½ cups self-raising flour, sifted
¾ cup caster sugar
4 oz (125g) butter, softened
grated zest of ½ orange
½ cup natural yogurt
¼ cup milk
2 eggs, lightly beaten
2 tablespoons freshly squeezed orange juice
3½ oz (100g) chocolate, roughly grated

Chocolate icing
1½ oz (45g) butter, softened
grated zest of ½ orange
¾ cup icing sugar, sifted
1½ tablespoons cocoa powder, sifted
4 teaspoons freshly squeezed orange juice

1 Preheat oven to 360°F (180°C).

2 Place flour, sugar, butter, orange zest, yogurt, milk, eggs and orange juice in a bowl and beat until ingredients are combined and batter is smooth. Fold in grated chocolate.

3 Spoon batter into a buttered 8 in (20cm) fluted ring tin and bake for 40–45 minutes or until cake is cooked when tested with a skewer. Stand cake in tin for 5 minutes before turning onto a wire rack to cool.

4 To make icing, place butter and orange zest in a heatproof bowl and beat until light and creamy. Add icing sugar, cocoa powder and orange juice and beat until combined. Add a little more orange juice if necessary. Place bowl over a saucepan of simmering water and cook, stirring constantly, for 2–3 minutes or until mixture is smooth and runny. Pour icing over cold cake.

Makes 1 cake • Preparation 45 minutes • Cooking 45 minutes

NEW YORK CHOCOLATE CAKE

4¾ oz (450g) semisweet (dark)
  chocolate
4¾ oz (450g) butter
1 cup espresso coffee
1 cup packed brown sugar
8 large eggs
8 oz (250g) fresh raspberries,
  to decorate

Raspberry sauce
1¾ lb (900g) fresh or frozen
  raspberries
juice of 1 lemon
2 tablespoons sugar

1 Preheat the oven to 360°F (180°C) and butter a 9½ in (24cm) non-stick cake tin or long non-stick loaf tin (not springform). Chop the chocolate and place in a large heatproof bowl.

2 In a small saucepan, bring the butter, espresso and brown sugar to the boil and simmer briefly. Pour the liquid over the chopped chocolate and allow to sit for a few minutes. Stir the ingredients gently to help the chocolate melt. Beat the eggs, then add to the chocolate mixture, whisking thoroughly.

3 Pour into the prepared cake tin, then place the tin in a large roasting pan or baking dish. Pour hot (not boiling) water into the roasting pan to reach halfway up the sides of the cake tin, then bake for 1 hour. Remove the cake from the water bath and chill overnight.

4 To make the raspberry sauce, purée the berries and their juice (if using frozen berries, thaw them first) with the lemon juice and sugar. Pour the sauce through a sieve then chill for up to 2 days.

5 The next day, remove the cake from the tin. If this is difficult, fill the kitchen sink with about 1½ in (4cm) of boiling water and dip the cake tin base in the water for a few seconds to loosen the cake. Run a knife or spatula around the tin then invert the cake onto a platter. Serve the cake with raspberry sauce and fresh raspberries.

Serves 12 • Preparation 10 minutes • Cooking 65 minutes

RICH DARK CHOCOLATE CAKE

15 oz (500g) milk chocolate, broken
  into pieces
14 oz (400g) unsalted butter
1½ cups superfine (caster) sugar
6 tablespoons all-purpose (plain) flour
6 large eggs, separated
pinch of salt
4 oz (125g) fresh raspberries, to serve
20 sprigs mint, to serve
¾ cup confectioner's (icing) sugar

Coating
6 tablespoons seedless
raspberry or cherry jelly (jam)
6 oz (200g) milk chocolate, broken into
  pieces
4 tablespoons cream
2 tablespoons pure confectioner's
  (icing) sugar

1 Preheat oven to 400°F (200°C). Butter two 8 x 4 in (20 x 10 in) loaf tins. Melt the chocolate with the butter, sugar and 3 tablespoons water in a bowl, over a saucepan of simmering water. Sift in flour and stir, then beat in egg yolks.

2 Place the egg whites into a bowl with a pinch of salt. Whisk with an electric whisk until the mixture forms stiff peaks. Fold 1 tablespoon of the whites into the chocolate mixture to loosen it, then fold in the remaining whites.

3 Divide the mixture between the tins and tap on the work surface to settle the contents. Bake for 45 minutes or until firm. Cool for 15 minutes in the tins. Turn out onto a cooling rack and leave for 2 hours or until cooled completely.

4 For the coating, heat the jelly with 3 tablespoons of water in a pan until dissolved. Brush over the tops and sides of the cakes. Melt the chocolate with 3 tablespoons of water in a bowl set over a pan of simmering water, then stir in the cream and sugar. Smooth over the top and sides of the cakes, then place in the refrigerator for 1 hour. Decorate with raspberries and mint and dust with confectioner's sugar. Serve with cream.

Serves 20 • Preparation 3 hrs 45 minutes • Cooking 50 minutes

106

MAGIC MICROWAVE CHOCOLATE CAKE

4 tablespoons all-purpose (plain) flour
4 tablespoons sugar
2 tablespoons cocoa
1 egg
3 tablespoons milk
3 tablespoons olive oil
3 tablespoons chocolate chips
a small splash of vanilla extract

1   Add flour, sugar and cocoa to a microwave proof mug, and mix well. Add the egg and mix thoroughly. Pour in the milk and oil and mix well. Add the chocolate chips and vanilla, and mix again.

2   Put the mug in the microwave and cook for 3 minutes at full power. The cake will rise over the top of the mug, something like a souffle. Allow to cool a little, and tip out onto a plate if desired, or eat with a spoon directly from the mug.

Serves 1 • Preparation 2 minutes • Cooking 3 minutes

CHOCOLATE SANDWICH CAKE

¾ cup flour self-rising (self-raising) flour, sifted
¼ teaspoon baking soda (bicarbonate of soda)
3 teaspoons cocoa powder, sifted
4 oz (125g) butter, softened
¾ cup superfine (caster) sugar
2 eggs, lightly beaten
1 cup sour cream
½ cup heavy (double) cream, whipped

Chocolate frosting
2 oz (60g) semisweet (dark) chocolate, chopped
1 oz (30g) unsalted butter

1 Place flour, bicarbonate of soda, cocoa powder, butter, sugar, eggs and sour cream in a large mixing bowl and beat until well combined and mixture is smooth.
2 Spoon batter into two greased and lined 8 in (20cm) sandwich tins and bake for 25–30 minutes or until cooked when tested with a skewer. Stand cakes in tins for 5 minutes before turning onto a wire rack to cool.
3 Sandwich cold cakes together with whipped cream.
4 For the frosting, put chocolate and butter in a small saucepan and cook over a low heat, stirring constantly, until melted. Cool slightly then spread over top of cake.

Serves 8 • Preparation 15 minutes • Cooking 30 minutes

CHOCOLATE HAZELNUT CAKE

9 oz (180g) cups semisweet (dark) chocolate, broken into pieces
6 eggs, separated
1 cup sugar
2 cups hazelnuts, toasted and roughly chopped
1 tablespoon dark rum
confectioner's (icing) sugar, sifted

1 Place the chocolate in a heatproof bowl set over a saucepan of simmering water and heat, stirring, until the chocolate melts. Remove the bowl from the pan and let it cool slightly.

2 Place the egg yolks and sugar in a bowl and beat until thick and pale. Fold the chocolate, hazelnuts and rum into the egg mixture.

3 Place the egg whites into a clean bowl and beat until stiff peaks form. Fold the egg whites into the chocolate mixture. Pour the mixture into a greased and lined 9 in (23cm) springform tin and bake for 50 minutes or until the cake is cooked when tested with a skewer. Cool the cake in the tin and dust it with confectioner's sugar just prior to serving.

Serves 8 • Preparation 30 minutes • Cooking 50 minutes

Sponges and
TEACAKES

For sunny morning teas and cosy afternoons

EGG YOLK SPONGE

¾ cup self-rising (self-raising) flour
1 tablespoon cornstarch (cornflour)
pinch of salt
4 egg yolks
½ cup superfine (caster) sugar
½ teaspoon vanilla extract
whipped cream

1 Preheat oven to 360°F (180°C).

2 Sift together the flour, cornstarch and salt. Beat yolks and 2 tablespoons hot water together until thick. Gradually add the sugar, beating well between each addition. Fold in sifted dry ingredients, extract and 2 tablespoons hot water. Pour into two buttered 7 in (18cm) round cake tins.

3 Bake in the centre of the oven for 20 minutes. When cold, fill with cream and decorate.

Makes 1 cake • Preparation 15 minutes • Cooking 20 minutes

MADEIRA CAKE

8 oz (250g) butter, softened
2 teaspoons vanilla extract
1 teaspoon finely grated lemon zest
2 cups superfine (caster) sugar
6 eggs
1½ cups all-purpose (plain) flour
1 cup self-rising (self-raising) flour
1 cup natural yogurt

Lemon frosting
1½ cups confectioner's (icing) sugar, sifted
1 tablespoon lemon juice
2 tablespoons butter, softened
2 tablespoons shredded coconut, toasted

1 Preheat oven to 320°F (160°C).

2 Place butter, vanilla extract and lemon zest in a bowl and beat until light and fluffy. Gradually add superfine sugar, beating well after each addition until mixture is creamy. Add eggs one at a time, beating well after each addition.

3 Sift together flour and self-rising flour. Fold flour mixture and yogurt, alternately, into butter mixture. Spoon batter into a buttered and lined 9 in (23cm) square cake tin and bake for 1 hour or until cake is cooked when tested with a skewer.

4 Stand in tin for 10 minutes before turning onto a wire rack to cool completely.

5 To make frosting, place confectioner's sugar, lemon juice and butter in a bowl and mix until smooth. Add a little more lemon juice if necessary. Spread frosting over cake and sprinkle with coconut.

Makes 1 cake • Preparation 30 minutes • Cooking 1 hour 10 minutes

CHERRY ALMOND CAKE

8 oz (250g) butter or margarine
1 cup superfine (caster) sugar
2 eggs
2 cups all-purpose (plain) flour
½ teaspoon ground cinnamon
½ teaspoon ground cloves
1 cup ground almonds
1 tablespoon gin
5 tablespoons cherry jelly (jam)
1 cup whipped cream

1 Preheat oven to 360°F (180°C).

2 Beat butter until soft, add sugar and continue beating until light and fluffy. Add eggs one at a time, beating well after each addition.

3 Sift flour, cinnamon, cloves and ground almonds together. Add to creamed mixture with gin, mixing with a wooden spoon until ingredients are well combined.

4 Spoon half the cake mixture into an 8 in (20cm) round deep cake tin that has been base-lined with buttered baking paper. Spread evenly with 3 tablespoons of the jelly, then spread evenly with remaining cake mixture.

5 Bake for 1 hour or until pale golden. Cool in the tin for 5 minutes, then turn out onto a wire rack to cool. Spread top of cake with cream and decorate with remaining jelly.

Makes 1 cake • Preparation 20 minutes • Cooking 1 hour

WASHINGTON SURPRISE

4 oz (125g) butter
½ cup superfine (caster) sugar
grated zest and juice of ¼ orange
2 eggs, beaten
1 cup self-rising (self-raising) flour, sifted with pinch of salt
10 oz (300g) canned cranberries, drained
10 oz (300g) canned blueberries, drained
2 tablespoons brandy

Meringue
5 egg whites
2 cups pure confectioner's (icing) sugar, sifted

1 Preheat the oven to 360°F (180°C).
2 Cream butter and sugar until light and fluffy. Add orange zest and juice and mix well. Add eggs, a little at a time, and beat thoroughly. Fold in the sifted flour and pour mixture into a buttered 7 in (18cm) round cake tin. Bake for 45–50 minutes.
3 When cooked, turn out onto an ovenproof plate and cut out a piece of cake from the base to make a hollow large enough to hold the berry mixture. Combine the fruit and brandy and fill the sponge. Replace cake piece and press down to form a flat lid.
4 To prepare the meringue, combine egg whites and confectioner's sugar in a bowl over hot water and whisk until stiff peaks are formed. Pipe the meringue decoratively on the sponge to encase completely. Place in the upper half of the oven at 500°F (260°C) or under a hot grill to brown.

Serves 8–10 • Preparation 35 minutes • Cooking 1 hour

SIMPLE SPONGE CAKE

1½ cups self-rising (self-raising) flour
1 cup superfine (caster) sugar
pinch of salt
4 oz (125g) butter, melted
½ cup milk
2 eggs, lightly beaten
1 teaspoon vanilla extract

1 Preheat oven to 360°F (180°C).
2 Sift flour, sugar and salt into a bowl. Combine butter and milk, stir into dry ingredients with eggs and vanilla. Beat until well combined. Pour into a buttered 7 in (18cm) round cake tin and bake in the centre of the oven for 30 minutes.

Makes 1 cake • Preparation 15 minutes • Cooking 30 minutes

AFTERNOON TEACAKE

2 oz (60g) butter
$\frac{1}{3}$ cup superfine (caster) sugar
1 egg, beaten
1$\frac{1}{2}$ cups self-rising (self-raising) flour
4–5 tablespoons milk
1 oz (30g) butter, melted
1 teaspoon superfine (caster) sugar, combined with
 2 teaspoons ground cinnamon

1 Preheat oven to 375°F (190°C).
2 Cream together butter and sugar. Add egg gradually, beating well.
  Fold in the flour and sufficient milk to make a soft batter. Place in a
  buttered 7 in (18cm) sandwich tin and bake in the upper half of the oven
  for 25–30 minutes. Allow to cool. Brush the surface with melted butter and
  sprinkle with superfine sugar and cinnamon.

Makes 1 cake • Preparation 10 minutes • Cooking 30 minutes

STRAWBERRY SHORTCAKE

8 oz (250g) butter
½ cup superfine (caster) sugar
2 eggs, lightly beaten
1 teaspoon vanilla extract
1½ cups all-purpose (plain) flour
½ cup cornstarch (cornflour)
1 tablespoon baking powder

Strawberry cream
1 quantity crème pâtissière filling (page 389)
¾ cup semi-whipped cream
1 cup sliced strawberries

1 Preheat oven 360°F (180°C).

2 Cream the butter and sugar until light and fluffy, add the eggs and vanilla and beat thoroughly. Sift together the flour, cornstarch and baking powder. Fold into the egg mixture and combine well. Place into three buttered 7 in (18cm) sandwich tins and bake in the centre of the oven for 20 minutes. Allow to cool.

3 To make the strawberry cream, combine the crème pâtissière, whipped cream and strawberries.

4 Fill the cake with strawberry cream and decorate the top with extra whipped cream and strawberries.

Makes 1 cake • Preparation 20 minutes • Cooking 20 minutes

CREAMY COCONUT CAKE

3¼ cups self-rising (self-raising) flour
pinch of salt
4 oz (125g) butter or margarine, cubed
1⅔ cups superfine (caster) sugar
1¼ cups desiccated coconut
4½ eggs, lightly beaten
¾ cup milk
1¼ cups heavy (double) cream
1 cup shredded coconut, toasted

Filling
2 cups coconut milk
½ cup desiccated coconut
2 tablespoons cornstarch (cornflour)
¼ cup milk
2 eggs, separated
2 tablespoons superfine (caster) sugar
2 tablespoons rum

1 Preheat oven to 360°F (180°C). Sift flour and salt together in a large bowl. Add butter and rub in with fingertips until mixture resembles fine breadcrumbs. Stir in the sugar and coconut and mix well. Add beaten eggs and milk, stirring until all ingredients are well combined.

2 Spoon mixture into a greased 10 in (25cm) deep round cake tin. Bake for 1 hour, then lower temperature to 320°F (160°C) for a further 10 minutes or until golden brown. Cool in the tin for 5 minutes, then turn out onto a wire rack to cool.

3 For the filling, place coconut milk and coconut in a heavy-based saucepan and bring to the boil. Place cornstarch and milk in a small bowl and mix until smooth. Add egg yolks, beat with a fork until well combined. Stir egg yolk mixture into coconut milk mixture and continue cooking over moderate heat until mixture thickens to a custard. Remove from heat and cool.

4 In a separate bowl, beat egg whites until stiff peaks form, gradually add superfine sugar and continue beating until mixture is thick and glossy. Fold egg white mixture and rum gently into cooled custard.

5 To assemble, cut cooled cake into three layers. Place one layer of the cake on a serving plate, spread with half the filling. Place a second layer of cake on top and spread with remaining filling, then finish with last layer of cake. To decorate, beat cream until thick and spread over top and sides of cake. Press coconut over cake.

Makes 1 cake • Preparation 45 minutes • Cooking 1 hour 15 minutes

VICTORIA SPONGE

8 oz (250g) butter
1¼ teaspoons vanilla extract
1 cup superfine (caster) sugar
4 eggs, lightly beaten
2 cups self-rising (self-raising) flour
pinch of salt

Filling
jelly (jam) of choice
whipped cream

To decorate
confectioner's (icing) sugar

1 Preheat oven to 375°F (190°C).

2 Butter two 8 in (20cm) round cake tins and line the base with buttered baking paper. Dust lightly with flour, tapping the tins to remove excess flour.

3 Place butter in a large bowl, add vanilla extract and beat until soft. Gradually add sugar and continue beating until mixture is light and fluffy. Slowly add beaten eggs to creamed mixture, beating well after each addition. If the eggs are added too quickly, the mixture will curdle. If curdling should occur, fold in a little of the measured flour and continue adding beaten eggs.

4 Sift flour and salt together and fold carefully into creamed mixture, mixing gently until well combined. Divide mixture evenly between the two tins and smooth the tops level with a spatula.

5 Bake for 30–35 minutes or until cakes spring back when the centre is pressed lightly with a finger. Remove cakes from the oven and place tins on a damp tea-towel. Leave for 2 minutes, then turn out onto a wire rack to cool. When cool, sandwich together with jelly and whipped cream. Decorate the top with sifted confectioner's sugar.

Makes 1 cake • Preparation 25 minutes • Cooking 35 minutes

MOCHA SPONGE

3 eggs, separated
½ cup superfine (caster) sugar
¾ cup self-rising (self-raising) flour
pinch of salt
1 tablespoon cocoa powder
1 teaspoon butter or margarine, melted
1 teaspoon instant coffee powder

Coffee cream
1 tablespoon instant coffee

1 tablespoon warm milk
½ cup heavy (double) cream
1–2 tablespoons confectioner's (icing) sugar, sifted

Glacé icing
1 cup confectioner's (icing) sugar, sifted
1 teaspoon butter or margarine
2 teaspoons instant coffee powder
few drops of vanilla extract

1 Preheat oven to 375°F (190°C). Butter two 7 in (18cm) sandwich tins and line the base of each tin with buttered baking paper. Beat egg whites until stiff peaks form, add sugar gradually and beat until thick and shiny. Add egg yolks one at a time, beating well after each addition. Sift flour, salt and cocoa together three times and lightly fold through egg mixture.

2 Combine butter, coffee and 2 tablespoons boiling water, pour around the edge of the mixture and, using a metal spoon, lightly fold in. Pour into prepared tins and bake for 20–25 minutes or until cake is firm to touch and starts coming away from the sides of the tin. Turn out onto a wire rack to cool.

3 To make the coffee cream, dissolve instant coffee in the warm milk. Whip cream until soft peaks form, then fold in the coffee mixture, sweeten to taste with the confectioner's sugar. Sandwich cakes together with coffee cream and place on a serving plate.

4 To make the glacé icing, place confectioner's sugar into a heatproof bowl over a pan of simmering water. Make a well in the centre of the confectioner's sugar, add the butter, coffee, vanilla extract and 1 tablespoon boiling water and stir slowly until well combined, smooth and shiny. Spread the top of the cake with the icing.

Makes 1 cake • Preparation 40 minutes • Cooking 25 minutes

CREAM FILLED SPONGE

3 eggs, separated
½ cup superfine (caster) sugar
1 cup self-rising (self-raising) flour, sifted
½ oz (15g) butter, melted
whipped cream to fill

1 Preheat oven to 360°F (180°C).
2 Beat the egg whites until stiff. Gradually add the sugar and beat until glossy. Fold in egg yolks, flour and butter, combined with 3 tablespoons boiling water. Pour into two buttered 8 in (20cm) round tins. Bake for 20–25 minutes. When cold, fill with cream and decorate.

Makes 1 cake • Preparation 15 minutes • Cooking 25 minutes

POWDER PUFFS

2 eggs, separated
pinch of salt
1/3 cup superfine (caster) sugar
few drops of vanilla extract
1/2 cup self-rising (self-raising) flour, sifted with 2 tablespoons
  cornstarch (cornflour)
whipped cream
confectioner's (icing) sugar, to dust

1 Preheat oven to 375°F (190°C).
2 Beat the egg whites and salt together until stiff. Add the sugar gradually and beat well between each addition until thick and glossy. Beat in the egg yolks and vanilla and fold in the sifted flours.
3 Spoon into buttered round-based patty cake tins and bake in the centre of the oven for 10–15 minutes. Allow to cool. Split in half, sandwich together with cream and dust with confectioner's sugar.

Note: Powder puffs may be spooned or piped onto baking paper on baking trays and cooked in the upper half of the oven for 7–10 minutes. Allow to cool. To remove from paper, slightly wet the back of the paper and peel off. Sandwich together as above.

Makes about 6–8 • Preparation 10 minutes • Cooking 15 minutes

ORANGE POPPYSEED CAKE

4 tablespoons poppy seeds
¼ cup orange juice
½ cup natural yogurt
7 oz (200g) butter, softened
1 tablespoon finely grated orange zest
1 cup superfine (caster) sugar
3 eggs
2 cups self-rising (self-raising) flour, sifted
2 tablespoons orange marmalade, warmed

1 Preheat oven to 360°F (180°C).
2 Place poppy seeds, orange juice and yogurt into a bowl, mix to combine and set aside to stand for 1 hour.
3 Place butter and orange zest in a bowl and beat until light and fluffy. Gradually add sugar, beating well after each addition until mixture is creamy.
4 Add eggs one at a time, beating well after each addition. Fold flour and poppy seed mixture, alternately, into butter mixture.
5 Spoon batter into a buttered 8 in (20cm) fluted ring tin and bake for 35–40 minutes or until cooked when tested with a skewer. Stand in tin for 5 minutes before turning onto a wire rack to cool completely. Brush with orange marmalade before serving.

Makes 1 cake • Preparation 1 hour 20 minutes • Cooking 40 minutes

GINGER FLUFF SPONGE

½ cup arrowroot
4 tablespoons plain flour
1 teaspoon cocoa powder
2 teaspoons ground ginger
1 teaspoon ground cinnamon
1 teaspoon cream of tartar

½ teaspoon baking soda
4 eggs, separated
½ cup caster sugar
1 tablespoon golden syrup, warmed
whipped cream
icing sugar, to dust

1 Preheat oven to 360°F (180°C).
2 Sift together the arrowroot, flour, cocoa, ginger, cinnamon, cream of tartar and baking soda.
3 Beat egg whites until stiff. Add sugar gradually, beating well between each addition. Beat in the egg yolks. Fold in sifted dry ingredients and golden syrup. Pour into two buttered 8 in (20cm) round cake tins. Bake in the centre of the oven for 20–22 minutes.
4 When cold, fill with cream and dust with icing sugar.

Makes 1 cake • Preparation 20 minutes • Cooking 20 minutes

MOCHA DESSERT CAKE

3½ oz (100g) cooking chocolate
5 oz (150g) butter
1 cup sugar
1 cup strong black coffee
1 cup all-purpose (plain) flour
¼ cup cornstarch (cornflour)
1 egg

1 Preheat oven to 320°F (160°C) and line the bottom of an 8 in (20cm) round cake tin with baking paper.

2 Mix chocolate, butter, sugar and coffee in a saucepan large enough to mix all the ingredients, and heat gently until butter and chocolate have melted and mixture is smooth.

3 Remove from heat. Sift in flour and cornstarch and add egg. Beat with a wooden spoon until smooth, then pour the mixture into the cake tin.

4 Bake for 50–60 minutes or until cake is firm. Stand in tin for 10 minutes before turning onto a cooling rack.

5 Serve dusted with cocoa powder and accompanied with fruit.

Serves 6–8 • Preparation 20 minutes • Cooking 60 minutes

PASSIONFRUIT SPONGE

4 eggs
¾ cup superfine (caster) sugar
1 cup all-purpose (plain) flour
4 teaspoons gluten-free baking
  powder
1 tablespoon margarine
Whipped cream, ricotta cheese or
  crème pâtissière to fill

Passionfruit frosting
2 tablespoons pure confectioner's
  (icing) sugar, sieved
1 tablespoon margarine
2 passionfruit, pulped scooped out

1 Preheat the oven to 360°F (180°C). Grease the sides of 2 x 8 in (20cm) flan tins and dust with gluten-free flour mixture. Line the bottom with baking paper. Do not use aluminium pans, as your sponge will not cook evenly (it will cook at the edges before the centre, giving you a dry result).

2 Hand whisk the eggs and superfine sugar over hot water until they are just warm and bubbly. Using an electric mixer, beat until the mixture is thick and creamy. Sift the flour and baking powder and fold into the egg mixture. Add the margarine to 3 tablespoons of boiling water and, when melted, pour the mixture down the inside of the bowl.

3 Fold the mixture with a wire whisk, being careful not to over mix as this will release the air and flatten the sponge. Pour into the tin and gently move the mixture with a spatula so that a small depression is made in the centre of the cake. Place in the centre of the preheated oven and cook for 15 minutes. Turn off the oven and stand for 5 minutes in the oven before removing and turning out.

4 To make the passionfruit frosting, combine the frosting ingredients with 1 tablespoon of boiling water and pour on the top of one cake. Fill the cake with whipped cream, softened creamed ricotta cheese or pâtissière custard.

Unfilled cakes freeze well if foil-wrapped. They will dry if only plastic-wrapped.

Serves 4 • Preparation 30 minutes • Cooking 20 minutes

MOCHA MOUSSE ROLL

4¾ oz (180g) semisweet (dark) chocolate, grated
2 oz (60g) butter
5 eggs, separated
2 tablespoons Tia Maria liqueur
⅓ cup superfine (caster) sugar
2 tablespoons cocoa powder, sifted
1 tablespoon instant coffee powder
1 cup heavy (double) cream

1 Preheat oven to 360°F (180°C). Lightly butter a Swiss roll tin and line with baking paper.

2 Melt chocolate and butter in a bowl over a bowl of simmering water and stir until smooth.

3 Beat in egg yolks one at a time, beating well after each addition. Stir in Tia Maria.

4 Beat egg whites in a small bowl until soft peaks form. Gradually add sugar, beating until mixture becomes thick and glossy. Fold in chocolate mixture, stir until well combined.

5 Spread mixture evenly into the Swiss roll tin. Bake for 30 minutes until firm. Turn out onto a sheet of greaseproof paper, sprinkle with sifted cocoa. Remove paper lining and allow to cool.

6 Combine coffee and 1 tablespoon boiling water, then cool. Beat cream until soft peaks form, stir in coffee mixture and 1 tablespoon extra Tia Maria. Spread evenly over cake and roll up lengthwise, using paper to help. Refrigerate until firm, then serve sliced.

Serves 8 • Preparation 40 minutes • Cooking 30 minutes

CONTINENTAL SPONGE

2 eggs
1/3 cup superfine (caster) sugar
1/2 cup all-purpose (plain) flour
2 teaspoon gluten-free baking powder
2 teaspoons margarine

1 Preheat the oven to 360°F (180°C). Grease an 8 in (20cm) flan tin and dust with flour or line with baking paper.

2 Whisk the eggs and superfine sugar over hot water until they are just warm and bubbly. Using an electric beater, beat until the mixture is thick and creamy but not stiff. Fold the flour and baking powder into the egg mixture.

3 Melt the margarine in 2 tablespoons of boiling water and pour down the inside of the bowl containing the batter. Turn the mixture with a wire whisk, being careful not to over-mix as this will release the air and flatten the sponge.

4 Pour into the tin and gently move the mixture with a spatula so that a small depression is made in the centre of the cake. Place in the centre of the oven and bake for 15 minutes. Stand for 5 minutes before turning out.

Serves 2–4 • Preparation 30 minutes • Cooking 20 minutes

CHOCOLATE ROLL

5 eggs, separated
¼ cup superfine (caster) sugar
¾ cup semisweet (dark) chocolate, melted and cooled
2 tablespoons all-purpose (plain) flour, sifted with
2 tablespoons cocoa powder and ¼ teaspoon baking powder

Chocolate filling
½ cup semisweet (dark) chocolate
⅔ cup heavy (double) cream

1 Place the egg yolks and sugar in a mixing bowl and beat until the mixture is thick and creamy. Beat in the chocolate, then fold in the flour mixture.

2 Beat the egg whites until stiff peaks form and fold into the chocolate mixture. Pour into a greased and lined 10 x 12 in (25 x 30cm) Swiss roll tin and bake for 12–15 minutes or until just firm. Turn onto a damp tea towel sprinkled with sugar and roll up from the short end. Set aside to cool.

3 To make the filling, place the chocolate and cream in a small saucepan and cook over a low heat until the chocolate melts and the mixture is well blended. Bring to the boil, remove from the heat and set aside to cool completely. When cold, place in a mixing bowl over ice and beat until thick and creamy.

4 Unroll the cake, spread with the filling and re-roll. To serve, cut into slices.

Note: A chocolate roll filled with chocolate cream makes a special afternoon tea treat or dessert. Irresistibly good to eat, these spectacular cakes are easy to make. Follow these step-by-step instructions for a perfect result every time.

Serves 8 • Preparation 45 minutes • Cooking 15 minutes

Fruit and Nut CAKES

Crunchy and juicy and all things fruity

DUNDEE CAKE

8 oz (250g) butter
1 teaspoon rum
1 cup superfine (caster) sugar
4 eggs
2 cups all-purpose (plain) flour
¼ cup cornstarch (cornflour)
1 teaspoon baking powder
1½ cups raisins
1½ cups currants
⅔ cup mixed peel
⅔ cup slivered almonds
⅓ cup glacé cherries, halved
2 teaspoons finely grated orange zest
1 tablespoon orange juice
¼ cup blanched almonds

1 Preheat oven to 300°F (150°C).

2 Place butter and rum in a bowl and beat until light and fluffy. Gradually beat in sugar and continue beating until mixture is creamy.

3 Beat in eggs one at a time and continue beating until mixture is combined. Sift flour, cornstarch and baking powder together, then fold into butter mixture.

4 Stir in raisins, currants, mixed peel, slivered almonds, cherries, orange zest and orange juice. Spoon mixture into a greased and lined deep 8 in (20cm) round cake tin. Arrange almonds in circles on top of cake and bake for 2½–3 hours or until cooked when tested with a skewer. Cool cake in tin before turning out and storing in an airtight container.

Makes 1 cake • Preparation 30 minutes • Cooking 3 hours

RICH FRUIT CAKE

2 lb (1kg) dried mixed fruit
1 cup dried dates, chopped
4 oz (125g) butter
¾ cup brown sugar
1 teaspoon ground cinnamon
½ cup brandy
2 eggs, lightly beaten
1 cup flour
½ cup self-rising (self-raising) flour

1 Preheat oven to 320°F (160°C).

2 Place mixed fruit, dates, butter, sugar, cinnamon and ½ cup of water in a large saucepan and cook over a medium heat, stirring until butter melts. Bring to the boil, reduce heat and simmer uncovered for 3 minutes.

3 Remove pan from heat and cool to room temperature.

4 Stir brandy and eggs into fruit mixture. Sift together flour and self-rising flour, add to fruit mixture and mix well to combine. Spoon batter into a buttered and lined 9 in (23cm) round tin and bake for 1¼–1½ hours or until cooked when tested with a skewer.

5 Allow to stand in tins for 10 minutes before turning onto a clean tea towel to cool completely.

Makes 1 cake • Preparation 30 minutes • Cooking 2 hours

FRUIT SHORTCAKE

2 cups self-rising (self-raising) flour, sifted
4 oz (125g) butter
½ cup superfine (caster) sugar, plus 2 extra tablespoons
1 egg, beaten
1 tablespoon lemon juice
7 oz (200g) fruit mincemeat (see note)
1 egg white, lightly beaten

1 Preheat oven to 360°F (180°C).

2 Place flour, butter and ½ cup sugar in a food processor and process until mixture resembles fine breadcrumbs. With machine running, slowly add egg and enough lemon juice to make a firm dough.

3 Turn onto a floured surface and knead briefly. Wrap dough in cling wrap and refrigerate for 30 minutes.

4 Divide dough in half. Roll out one half large enough to cover the base and sides of a buttered 8 in (20cm) sandwich tin. Spread fruit mincemeat over base.

5 Roll our remaining dough large enough to cover mincemeat. Press edges together firmly. Brush with egg white and sprinkle with remaining sugar. Bake for 30–35 minutes or until cooked.

6 Stand for 10 minutes before turning onto a wire rack to cool completely.

Note: Mincemeat is a combination of dried fruits, distilled spirits and spices.

Serves 8 • Preparation 30 minutes • Cooking 45 minutes

COFFEE AND WALNUT CAKE

1 cup all-purpose (plain) flour
¾ cup self-rising (self-raising) flour
1 teaspoon baking soda (bicarbonate of soda)
1 teaspoon mixed spice
½ teaspoon ground nutmeg
½ teaspoon salt
1 cup walnuts, roughly chopped
1 tablespoon instant coffee
½ cup superfine (caster) sugar
½ cup honey

2 eggs, lightly beaten
4 oz (125g) butter, melted and cooled
¼ cup milk

Coffee butter cream
5 oz (150g) butter
3 cups confectioner's (icing) sugar, sifted
3 tablespoons instant coffee
chopped walnuts to decorate

1 Preheat oven to 360°F (180°C).

2 Sift the flours, baking soda, spices and salt into a large bowl. Add the walnuts.

3 In a separate bowl, combine instant coffee, sugar, honey and 2 tablespoons of hot water.

4 Make a well in the centre of the flour mixture, add the eggs, butter, milk and coffee mixture and stir lightly until combined. Spoon the cake mixture into two buttered 8 in (20cm) shallow cake tins that have been base-lined with baking paper and bake for 30–35 minutes or until golden brown.

5 To make the coffee butter cream, beat butter and confectioner's sugar in a small bowl until light and fluffy. Dissolve coffee in 3 tablespoons of hot water, allow to cool before beating into creamed butter mixture.

6 Cool the cakes in the tin. Place one of the cakes on a serving plate. Spread or pipe half of coffee butter cream over cake and place other cake on top. Spoon half of the remaining coffee butter cream smoothly over cake and decorate with extra walnuts.

Makes 1 cake • Preparation 30 minutes • Cooking 40 minutes

STRAWBERRY HAZELNUT TORTE

5 eggs
½ cup sugar
4 tablespoons all-purpose (plain) flour
1 teaspoon coffee powder
1 teaspoon ground allspice
3 oz (90g) ground hazelnuts

Filling and topping
20 whole hazelnuts
5 oz (150g) chocolate, melted with 2 oz (60g) copha
2 cups heavy (double) cream
4 tablespoons brandy
½ cup confectioner's (icing) sugar, sifted
1 lb (500g) strawberries, sliced

1 Preheat oven to 360°F (180°C).

2 Beat eggs until light and fluffy, gradually add sugar, beating well between each addition. Sift together the flour, coffee powder and allspice. Fold hazelnuts and sifted ingredients gently into egg mixture. Pour evenly into two square well-buttered and lined 9 in (23cm) sandwich tins.

3 Bake in the centre of the oven for 10–15 minutes. Remove from oven, cool, then replace in oven for a further 5 minutes. Cut tortes in half to form four oblong layers.

4 To make the filling and topping, dip hazelnuts into chocolate mixture and allow to set. Spread remaining chocolate evenly over three torte layers.

5 Whip together the cream, brandy and confectioner's sugar. Add the strawberries to half the cream mixture. Mix thoroughly and spread onto the three chocolate covered layers. Place these layers on top of each other, finishing with the uncovered layer. Spread remaining cream over the assembled torte and decorate with cream, chocolate hazelnuts and extra strawberries. Refrigerate for 2 hours before serving.

Makes 1 cake • Preparation 30 minutes, plus 2 hours refrigeration
• Cooking 20 minutes

ORANGE DESSERT CAKE

¼ oz (7g) sachet dry yeast
¾ cup fresh orange juice
7 oz (200g) butter or margarine
¾ cup superfine (caster) sugar
finely grated zest of 1 orange
3 eggs
2¼ cups self-rising (self-raising) flour
1¼ cups heavy (double) cream,
 whipped

strawberries and orange segments
 to decorate

Syrup
¾ cup orange juice
¾ cup confectioner's (icing) sugar,
 sifted
¼ cup orange liqueur

1 Preheat oven to 360°F (180°C). Butter a 9 in (23cm) deep ring tin.

2 Mix yeast and orange juice together in a small bowl. Beat butter until soft, add sugar and orange zest and continue beating until mixture is light and fluffy. Add the eggs one at a time, beating well after each addition.

3 Sift flour, add to the creamed mixture with the yeast and orange juice mixture, stirring gently until all ingredients are well combined.

4 Spoon mixture into the prepared tin. Bake for 35–40 minutes or until a skewer inserted in the centre comes out clean. While cake is cooking, make syrup.

5 To make the syrup, place orange juice and confectioner's sugar in a small saucepan, cook over moderate heat, stirring until liquid boils. Remove pan from the heat and cool, stir in liqueur.

6 When cake is cooked, remove from the oven, leave in the tin and pour over the cooled syrup. When syrup has been absorbed, turn cake out onto a serving plate. Allow to cool.

7 To decorate, spoon whipped cream into centre of cake. Decorate with strawberries and orange segments.

Makes 1 cake • Preparation 30 minutes • Cooking 40 minutes

STRAWBERRY MERINGUE

6 egg whites
1¾ cups superfine (caster) sugar
1 teaspoon lemon juice
¼ cup ground toasted almonds
8 oz (250g) strawberries, halved
warm strawberry jelly (jam)

Filling
3 oz (90g) strawberry Jell-O® crystals
1 cup heavy (double) cream
2 tablespoons chocolate liqueur
¾ cup roughly chopped strawberries
2 oz (60g) chocolate, melted and
   cooled

1 Preheat oven to 280°F (140°C). Lightly butter a baking tray and dust lightly with cornstarch. Trace an 8 in (20cm) circle on a piece of baking paper.

2 Beat egg whites in a bowl until stiff peaks just form. Gradually add the sugar and continue beating until mixture is thick and glossy. Gently fold in lemon juice.

3 Fill a large piping bag fitted with a plain ½ in (1.2cm) tube with meringue mixture and pipe meringue onto paper circle, starting in the centre and filling in completely. Alternatively, spread the mixture out with a spatula to form a round. Pipe large rosettes around meringue base.

4 Sprinkle almonds over base of meringue case and gently swirl into the mixture using a fork. Bake for 1¼ hours or until crisp, then turn oven off and leave in oven to dry out.

5 For the filling, place Jell-O® crystals and 1 cup boiling water in a heatproof bowl, stir until crystals dissolve. Chill until just beginning to set around the edge. Whip cream and liqueur together in a bowl until thick, and gently fold into Jell-O® with chopped strawberries. Spread melted chocolate over base of meringue shell, and spoon cream mixture on top.

6 To decorate, top with halved strawberries. Brush strawberries with warm strawberry jelly and refrigerate until ready to serve.

Makes 1 cake • Preparation 50 minutes • Cooking 1 hour 15 minutes

HAZELNUT PRALINE GATEAU

4 tablespoons hazelnuts, plus extra to decorate
⅓ cup self-rising (self-raising) flour
2 teaspoons instant coffee powder
1 teaspoon ground allspice
4 eggs, separated
½ cup superfine (caster) sugar

Hazelnut praline
1 cup superfine (caster) sugar
4 tablespoons hazelnuts
2¼ cup confectioner's (icing) sugar, sifted
1 lb (500g) cream cheese, at room temperature

1 Preheat oven to 360°F (180°C).

2 Butter two x 8 in (20cm) round cake tins, line the bases with baking paper and dust each with a tablespoon of flour, turning each tin to coat the base and sides evenly. Shake off any excess.

3 Place hazelnuts in a blender or food processor and blend until finely ground. Sift flour, coffee powder and allspice together onto a sheet of baking paper.

4 Beat the egg whites until stiff. Gradually add the sugar and beat until glossy. Fold in egg yolks, flour and hazelnut mixture, combined with 3 tablespoons boiling water. Pour into prepared tins. Bake for 20–25 minutes.

5 To make the hazelnut praline, place the superfine sugar and hazelnuts together in a heavy-based saucepan over a very low heat, cook without stirring for about 5–6 minutes until the sugar dissolves and turns golden. Pour immediately onto a baking tray covered with well-buttered aluminium foil and allow to set. Break up with a heavy spoon, then use a food processor or rolling pin to crush to a fine praline. Beat together the confectioner's sugar and cream cheese until light and smooth, then fold in the praline.

6 Cut each sponge in half, spread each half with half the hazelnut praline, stack the pieces of sponge on top of each other and use the remaining praline as frosting. Decorate with whole hazelnuts.

Serves 8 • Preparation 35 minutes • Cooking 30 minutes

PECAN GATEAU

7 oz (200g) butter or margarine
2 teaspoons vanilla extract
1⅓ cups superfine (caster) sugar
3 eggs, separated
1 cup chopped pecans
2 cups self-rising (self-raising) flour
2 teaspoons baking powder
1 teaspoon mixed spice
1 teaspoon ground nutmeg
¾ cup milk

Maple cream
8 oz (250g) butter, cut into pieces
2½ cups confectioner's (icing) sugar, sifted
1 tablespoon maple syrup

To decorate
chopped pecan nuts
pecan nuts, extra

1 Preheat oven to 360°F (180°C). Beat butter and vanilla extract until soft, add sugar and continue beating until light and fluffy. Add egg yolks and pecans and beat until well combined.

2 Sift flour, baking powder, mixed spice and nutmeg together, add to creamed mixture with milk and stir lightly until ingredients are well combined.

3 Beat egg whites until soft peaks form and gently fold into cake mixture. Spoon cake mixture evenly into two buttered 9 in (23cm) round cake tins, base lined with buttered baking paper. Bake for 35 minutes or until golden brown. Cool in the tin for 10 minutes, then turn out onto a wire rack to cool.

4 To make the maple cream, beat butter until soft and light, add confectioner's sugar and maple syrup and continue beating until light and fluffy. If mixture is too thick, add a little extra maple syrup.

5 To assemble, cut each cake in half and place one half on a serving plate. Spread a little of the maple cream evenly over the cake, top with another layer of the cake. Continue sandwiching cake layers together with the maple cream until the cake is assembled. Using a spatula or palette knife, spread remaining maple cream over top and sides of the cake, press extra chopped pecans around the sides and decorate with whole pecans on top.

Makes 1 gateau • Preparation 35 minutes • Cooking 35 minutes

GLAZED CHERRY GATEAU

3 sheets ready-rolled puff pastry
½ cup redcurrant jelly (jam), warmed
⅓ cup confectioner's (icing) sugar, sifted
3 teaspoons lemon juice
15 oz (425g) canned, pitted, dark

cherries, drained and liquid reserved
1 tablespoon cornstarch (cornflour)
2 tablespoons sugar
pinch of cinnamon
2 cups heavy (double) cream

1 Preheat oven to 360°F (180°C). Cut a 9 in (23cm) circle out of each of the pastry sheets. Place the pastry circles on lightly dampened baking trays and bake for 10–12 minutes or until pastry is lightly browned on top. Cool on trays. When cool, remove from the trays and spread the best-looking pastry round with the warmed redcurrant jelly.

2 In a bowl, mix the confectioner's sugar and lemon juice together until smooth. Drizzle over the top of the jelly-glazed pastry circle and set aside.

3 Mix a little of the reserved cherry liquid and with cornstarch until smooth, and pour into a saucepan with the remaining cherry liquid, 1 tablespoon of sugar and the cinnamon. Bring to the boil and cook, stirring constantly, until mixture has thickened, about 3 minutes. Remove from the heat and stir in the pitted cherries. Cool.

4 Place one round of pastry on a serving plate, spread with half the cooled cherry mixture. Whip the cream with the remaining sugar until soft peaks form.

5 Spoon half of the whipped cream over the cherries. Top with another layer of pastry. Spread with remaining cherry mixture. Spread remaining cream over the cherries and arrange glazed pastry round on top of cream.

Makes 1 gateau • Preparation 35 minutes • Cooking 15 minutes

BLACK FOREST CAKE

1 tablespoon vinegar
1 cup evaporated milk
1½ cups all-purpose (plain) flour
pinch of salt
½ cup cocoa powder
1½ teaspoons baking soda
  (bicarbonate of soda)
1¼ cups superfine (caster) sugar
7 oz (200g) butter or margarine, melted

1 teaspoon vanilla extract
2 eggs
8 oz (250g) cooking chocolate
grated maraschino or glacé cherries

Filling
24 oz (680g) jar morello cherries, pitted
⅓ cup cherry liqueur
2⅓ cups cream
3 tablespoons superfine (caster) sugar

1 Preheat oven to 360°F (180°C). Add vinegar to milk, stir well, set aside.

2 Sift the flour, salt, cocoa, baking soda and sugar into a bowl. Pour in the melted butter and half the soured milk, and beat well for 2 minutes.

3 Add vanilla, eggs and milk, beat for a further 2 minutes. Pour mixture into two buttered 8 in (20cm) tins base-lined with baking paper. Bake 35 minutes or until a skewer comes out clean. Allow to cool in the tins.

4 To make the filling, drain morello cherries, reserving the syrup in which they are packed. Measure ½ cup of the cherry syrup and place in a saucepan with the cherry liqueur. Bring mixture to the boil, then lower heat and simmer for 3 minutes. Remove from heat and allow to cool.

5 Beat cream with the sugar until thick. Cut each cake in half and place one half on a serving plate. Brush liberally with cherry syrup, then spread over ½ cup of the whipped cream. Scatter with ⅓ of the cherries, then top with another round of cake. Brush with syrup, spread with cream, scatter another ⅓ of the cherries. Assemble the next layer, finishing with the last round of cake. Brush with cherry syrup, then spread the remaining cream over the top and sides of the cake.

6 Press grated chocolate on the top and sides of the cake. Decorate with maraschino or glacé cherries. Chill for several hours.

Makes 1 gateau • Preparation 45 minutes • Cooking 35 minutes

CHERRY FILLED ALMOND CAKE

3 eggs
1 teaspoon almond extract
¼ cup superfine (caster) sugar
4 tablespoons self-rising (self-raising) flour, sifted with 2 tablespoons cornstarch (cornflour)
2 oz (60g) ground almonds

Cherry filling
3½ oz (100g) cherry conserve
8 oz (250g) ricotta cheese

Cream topping
3 tablespoons cherry conserve
6 oz (170g) cream cheese
2 tablespoons confectioner's (icing) sugar, sifted
¼ cup heavy (double) cream
2 oz (60g) flaked almonds, toasted

1 Preheat oven to 360°F (180°C). Place eggs, almond extract and sugar in a mixing bowl and beat until very thick and creamy (about 10 minutes). Fold in flour mixture and almonds. Pour into buttered and lined 9 in (23cm) round cake tin. Bake in oven for 20–25 minutes, or until sponge is golden and springs back when gently touched with fingertips. Carefully turn out onto a wire rack to cool. When cold, cut into three even layers.

2 To make filling, place cherry conserve and ricotta cheese in a food processor or blender and process until smooth.

3 Place one sponge layer on serving plate and spread with half the filling. Top with another sponge layer and remaining filling. Place remaining sponge layer on top and refrigerate for 10 minutes.

4 To make topping, place cherry conserve, cream cheese and confectioner's sugar in a food processor or blender and process until smooth. Pour in cream and continue to process until smooth and thick. Spread topping over top and sides of gateau. Press flaked almonds around side of gateau and refrigerate until ready to serve.

Serves 8 • Preparation 40 minutes • Cooking 25 minutes

PEAR UPSIDE DOWN PUDDING

¼ cup raw sugar
2 x 15 oz (440g) canned pear halves, drained, with 1 cup syrup reserved
8 oz (250g) butter, softened
2 cups self-rising (self-raising) flour
1 cup superfine (caster) sugar
4 eggs
1 cup chopped walnuts
¼ cup maple syrup

1 Preheat oven to 360°F (180°C).
2 Sprinkle base of a deep buttered and lined 9 in (23cm) round cake tin with raw sugar. Cut pear halves in half to form quarters and arrange cut-side up, over base.
3 Place butter, flour, sugar and eggs in a food processor and process until smooth. Stir in walnuts. Carefully spoon batter over fruit in tin and bake for 1–1¼ hours or until cooked when tested with a skewer.
4 Place maple syrup and reserved pear juice in a saucepan over a medium heat and cook until syrup is reduced by half.
5 Turn pudding onto a serving plate and pour over syrup. Serve with cream or ice cream.

Serves 8 • Preparation 20 minutes • Cooking 1 hour 15 minutes

CITRUS DELICIOUS PUDDING

1 cup superfine (caster) sugar
4 oz (125g) butter, softened
½ cup self-rising (self-raising) flour
1 tablespoon finely grated lemon zest
1 tablespoon finely grated orange zest
2 tablespoons lemon juice
2 tablespoons orange juice
2 eggs, separated
1 cup milk

1 Preheat oven to 360°F (180°C).
2 Place sugar and butter in a bowl and beat until light and fluffy. Stir in flour, lemon and orange zests, and lemon and orange juices.
3 Place egg yolks and milk in a bowl and whisk to combine. Stir into citrus mixture.
4 Place egg whites in a bowl and beat until stiff peaks form, then fold into batter. Spoon batter into a buttered 4-cup capacity ovenproof dish. Place dish in a baking pan with enough boiling water to come halfway up the sides of dish. Bake for 45 minutes or until cooked.

Serves 6 • Preparation 20 minutes • Cooking 45 minutes

GRAND MARNIER SOUFFLE

½ cup orange juice
1 teaspoon grated orange zest
¾ cup cooked long-grain rice
4 egg yolks
1 tablespoon superfine (caster) sugar, plus ⅓ cup
1 tablespoon cornstarch (cornflour)
1¼ cups milk
4 tablespoons Grand Marnier
5 egg whites

1 Preheat oven to 430°F (220°C).

2 Place orange juice, zest and rice in a saucepan and bring to the boil. Reduce heat and allow to simmer, stirring occasionally, until all liquid has been absorbed. Set aside.

3 Whisk together egg yolks, 1 tablespoon superfine sugar and cornstarch. Heat milk in a saucepan until just at boiling point. Add to egg yolk mixture, whisk, then return mixture to saucepan. Stir over medium heat until custard boils and thickens. Reduce heat and simmer for 3–4 minutes, stirring constantly. Remove from heat. Stir in Grand Marnier and rice mixture. Cool slightly.

4 Beat egg whites until stiff peaks form. Add extra sugar, a tablespoon at a time, beating after each addition. Stir a little beaten egg white into rice custard then lightly fold in remaining whites. Spoon into prepared soufflé dish. Bake for 20–25 minutes until soufflé is puffed and golden. Serve immediately.

Serves 4 • Preparation 30 minutes • Cooking 40 minutes

APPLE AND RAISIN SPICE RING

1 teaspoon salt
2 tablespoons superfine (caster) sugar
1 tablespoon gelatin
2 oz (60g) mashed potato (see note)
1 tablespoon dried yeast
1$\frac{2}{3}$ cup fine flour
1 teaspoon ground ginger
1 teaspoon mixed spice
1 teaspoon ground cinnamon

2 eggs
1 cup raisins
1 medium apple, peeled and chopped

Topping
2 cups pure confectioner's (icing) sugar
3 tablespoons margarine
walnuts, to decorate

1 Preheat oven to 360°F (180°C). Grease an 8 in (20cm) ring pan. Place 7 oz (200ml) of cold water in a glass bowl. Add salt, superfine sugar and gelatin. Let stand for 1 minute to soften gelatin. Heat the gelatin mixture until clear.

2 Whisk the mashed potato into the warm gelatin mixture. Stir in the yeast and whisk slightly. Let stand for 3 minutes. Combine flour and spices. Lightly whisk the eggs with an electric mixer.

3 Tip the dry ingredients into the yeast mixture and beat in the eggs. Beat the mixture for 1 minute with the electric mixer. Pour a quarter of the mixture into the pan and spread over the base. Sprinkle a quarter of the raisins and apple over the mixture and top with more batter.

4 Sprinkle over the remaining fruit and cover with more mixture. Leave to stand for 15 minutes until a few bubbles appear. Place in the centre of the oven and bake for 35 minutes. Remove from the oven and wrap in a clean tea towel to cool.

5 Cream together confectioner's sugar and margarine, adding a little hot water if necessary. Ice the cake when cool, and decorate with walnuts.

One medium-sized potato produces approximately 2 oz (60g) mashed potato.

Serves 4–6 • Preparation 30 minutes • Cooking 35 minutes

LEMON DELICIOUS PUDDING

2 tablespoons margarine
1 cup sugar
zest and juice of 2 lemons
4 eggs, separated
3 tablespoons bread (strong plain) flour
1 cup milk

1 Preheat the oven to 360°F (180°C). Grease a small casserole dish with margarine. Cream together the margarine, sugar, zest and egg yolks.
2 Add the sifted flours, milk and juice – stir to combine. Separately beat the egg whites until stiff and fold into the mixture.
3 Pour into the prepared casserole dish and place in the centre of the oven.
4 Cook for approximately 20–25 minutes until the sponge is firm to touch. As there is custard underneath the sponge, the pudding will be a little wobbly when it is cooked. Serve warm with cream or ice cream.

Serves 4 • Preparation 20 minutes • Cooking 25 minutes

PLUM JAM PUDDING

margarine to grease the basin
2 tablespoons plum jelly (jam)
2 oz (60g) butter
¼ cup sugar
1 egg
½ cup all-purpose (plain) flour
1 teaspoon gluten-free baking powder
1 tablespoon milk

1 Place a saucepan that will fit a 5 x 2 in (13 x 6cm) deep fluted pudding basin, on to boil with enough water to come halfway up the pudding basin. Make sure that you have a tight fitting lid for the saucepan.

2 Grease the pudding basin well with margarine, and cut a piece of greaseproof paper large enough to fit the top of the basin. The paper should be larger than the basin so that it will not let any water in when the pudding is steaming.

3 Place the plum jelly in the bottom of the greased pudding basin. Cream the butter, sugar and egg together until fluffy. Fold in the sifted flour and baking powder. Stir in the milk and pour into the pudding basin. Lower the pudding into the boiling water. Loosely lay the greaseproof paper on top of the pudding.

4 Place the lid on the saucepan and keep the water boiling for about 40 minutes. When cooked, turn the pudding out onto a plate and serve with custard or ice cream.

Serves 3 • Preparation 25 minutes • Cooking 40 minutes

LEMON AND HAZELNUT CAKE

¾ cup butter, softened
¾ cup superfine (caster) sugar
1 cup self-rising (self-raising) flour
1 cup ground hazelnuts
3 eggs
¼ cup cream

Lemon syrup
2 teaspoons grated lemon zest
juice of 2 lemons
½ cup superfine (caster) sugar

1 Grease a 10 in (25cm) fluted tube tin.
2 Place the butter, sugar, flour, hazelnuts, eggs, and cream into a large bowl. Using an electric mixer, beat until smooth, for 2–3 minutes.
3 Pour the mixture into a prepared cake tin and bake in a preheated oven for 40–45 minutes.
4 Before the cake is done, make the lemon syrup. Combine all the ingredients in a saucepan and stir over a low heat until the sugar is dissolved. Bring to the boil, remove from the heat and pour into a jug when ready to use.
5 When cake is baked, remove from oven and turn out onto a wire rack. Place the cake on a cooling rack over a tray. Using a skewer, lightly prick the cake.
6 Pour the hot lemon syrup evenly over the hot cake. Cool and serve with whipped cream if desired.

Note: You may like to freeze swirls of fresh cream on a baking tray. When frozen, transfer them carefully to a container for storage. They are ideal for garnishing.

Serves 6–8 • Preparation 10 minutes • Cooking 45 minutes

194

MOCHA WALNUT CAKE

1 x batter for butter cake (page 29)
$^{1}/_{3}$ cup cocoa, or to taste
2 eggs
2 teaspoons instant coffee powder
$^{2}/_{3}$ cup water
3 tablespoons margarine
¼ cup chopped walnuts

Coffee glacé topping
1 teaspoon coffee powder
2 teaspoons of hot water
2 cups sifted icing sugar
1 tablespoon margarine, softened

1 Make up the cake batter as directed. Dissolve the coffee in the water and fold the margarine, cocoa and walnuts through the batter. Spoon the mixture into a lightly greased 10 in (25cm) fluted tube tin.

2 Bake in an oven at 180°C for 40 minutes or until cooked when tested. Cool for 5 minutes in the tin before turning out. Cool.

3 To make the coffee glacé topping, dissolve the coffee in the water. Blend into the confectioner's sugar and margarine and mix well. Top the cool cake.

Serves 6–8 • Preparation 30 minutes • Cooking 15 minutes

ARABIAN DATE CAKE

1¼ cups chopped dates
1 cup water
1 teaspoon instant coffee powder
½ cup margarine
½ cup brown sugar
¼ cup honey
2 eggs
¾ cup semisweet (dark) chocolate, melted
2 cups self-rising (self-raising) flour, sifted

1 Combine the dates, water and coffee in a small saucepan. Cook gently until the dates are tender and the liquid has been absorbed.

2 Mash the dates with a fork. Cream together the margarine, sugar and honey until light and creamy. Beat the eggs in, one at a time, beating well between each addition. Add the melted chocolate.

3 Fold in the sifted flour with the date mixture. Mix well. Spoon the mixture into a lightly greased 10 in (25cm) fluted cake tin. Bake in a pre-heated oven for 45–50 minutes or until cooked when tested.

4 Cool for 5 minutes in the tin. Serve warm or cold, spread with margarine or coffee cream cheese.

Serves 6–8 • Preparation 15 minutes • Cooking 50 minutes

Fruit and nut cakes   199

PASSIONFRUIT DESSERT CAKE

½ cup margarine
¾ cup superfine (caster) sugar
grated zest of 1 orange
2 eggs
1¼ cups self-rising (self-raising) flour, sifted
½ cup fresh or canned passionfruit pulp (see note)
icing sugar to dust
whipped cream

Passionfruit sauce
½ cup fresh or canned passionfruit pulp
1 tablespoon icing sugar
1 tablespoon orange juice

1 Cream together the margarine, sugar and orange zest. Beat in the eggs one at a time, beating well between each addition.

2 Fold in the sifted flour, along with the passionfruit pulp. Spoon the mixture into a deep, lightly greased 10 in (25cm) round cake tin. Bake in a pre-heated oven for 40–45 minutes.

3 To make the passionfruit sauce, combine the passionfruit pulp, sugar and orange juice.

4 Serve cake warm, dusted with sifted confectioner's sugar and accompanied by the passionfruit sauce and whipped cream.

Note: Fresh passionfruit may not always be readily available. Canned passionfruit pulp may be used instead. Most canned passionfruit pulp is strained to remove the seeds, but retains its taste.

Serves 6 • Preparation 10 minutes • Cooking 45 minutes

Yummy
CHEESECAKES

Marvellous mixtures on crumbly bases

UNBAKED CHEESECAKE

1⅓ cup plain sweet cookies (biscuits), crushed
1½ oz (50g) butter, melted
1 lb (500g) cottage cheese or cream cheese
½ cup superfine (caster) sugar
2 tablespoons lemon juice
¼ cup milk
1 cup heavy (double) cream
1 tablespoon gelatin
2 egg whites

1 Combine crushed cookies and butter together and press onto the base of a 8½ in (22cm) springform tin. Refrigerate while preparing filling.

2 Cream together the cheese and sugar until smooth. Beat in lemon juice and milk, then gently fold in cream.

3 Sprinkle the gelatin onto 2 tablespoons hot water and stir briskly until dissolved to a clear golden liquid. Add to cheese mixture.

4 Whip egg whites until stiff peaks form. Fold into cheese mixture. Pour into prepared tin. Refrigerate until firm.

5 Decorate with whipped cream and thin lemon twists.

Serves 8 • Preparation 30 minutes

BLACK FOREST CHEESECAKE

1½ cups graham cracker (digestive biscuit) crumbs
2 oz (60g) butter, melted
¼ cup cocoa powder
1¾ cups sugar
1½ lb (750g) cream cheese
4 eggs
¼ cup amaretto
¼ cup maraschino cherry juice
4½ oz (125g) semisweet chocolate, melted
½ cup sour cream

1 Combine the graham cracker crumbs, butter, cocoa and ¼ cup sugar and mix well. Firmly press into the bottom and 1 in (2.5cm) up the sides of an 8½ in (22cm) springform tin. Set aside.

2 Preheat oven to 360°F (180°C).

3 Beat cream cheese with an electric mixer until fluffy. Gradually add remaining sugar and mix well.

4 Add eggs one at a time, beating well after each addition, then add the amaretto and cherry juice until well blended.

5 Pour into crust and bake for 1 hour.

6 When cooked, remove from oven and allow to cool for 2–3 hours on a wire rack.

7 While cake is cooling, combine melted chocolate and sour cream, and when cake is cool, spread evenly over top of cheesecake.

8 Chill in refrigerator overnight. Before serving, garnish with whipped cream and maraschino cherries.

Serves 10 • Preparation 35 minutes • Cooking 60 minutes

ALMOND CHEESECAKE

¾ cup caster sugar
2 oz (60g) butter, softened
1 lb (500g) cream cheese
¼ cup plain flour, sifted
2 tablespoons honey
5 eggs, separated
½ cup double cream
1 teaspoon vanilla extract

2½ oz (75g) blanched almonds, finely chopped

Brown sugar topping
¼ cup brown sugar
3 tablespoons finely chopped blanched almonds
1 teaspoon ground cinnamon

1 Preheat oven to 300°F (150°C).

2 To make topping, place brown sugar, almonds and cinnamon in a bowl and mix to combine. Set aside.

3 Place caster sugar and butter in a bowl and beat until light and fluffy. Beat in cream cheese and continue beating until mixture is creamy. Beat in flour, honey and egg yolks and continue beating until well combined. Fold in cream and vanilla extract. Place egg whites in a bowl and beat until stiff peaks form. Fold egg whites and almonds into cream cheese mixture.

4 Spoon mixture into a buttered and lined 10 in (25cm) springform tin. Sprinkle with topping and bake for 1½ hours or until just firm. Turn off oven and leave cheesecake in oven to cool.

Serves 8 • Preparation 30 minutes • Cooking 1 hour 30 minutes

RICOTTA CHEESECAKE

6½ oz (180g) graham crackers (digestive biscuits), finely crushed
3 lb (1⅓ kg) ricotta, drained
2 cups sugar
8 egg yolks
½ cup all-purpose (plain) flour, sifted
zest of 1 lemon
1 teaspoon vanilla extract
8 egg whites
½ cup heavy (double) cream, whipped

1 Preheat oven to 430°F (220°C).

2 Sprinkle a 12 in (30cm) springform tin with the graham cracker crumbs.

3 Beat ricotta until smooth, gradually add three-quarters of the sugar, then add egg yolks one at a time, mixing well after each addition. Beat in flour, lemon zest and vanilla.

4 Beat egg whites with remaining sugar. Fold whipped cream and egg whites into ricotta mixture and turn into prepared tin. Bake for 10 minutes, lower temperature to 360°F (180°C) and bake for 1 hour. Turn off heat and allow to cool in oven with door closed. Dust with confectioner's sugar before serving.

Serves 12 • Preparation 35 minutes • Cooking 1 hour 10 minutes

FOREST FRUIT CHEESECAKE

Base

2 oz (60g) graham crackers (digestive biscuits), finely crushed
1 oz (30g) butter, melted
¼ cup sugar

Filling

1 lb (500g) cream cheese, softened
1 tablespoon lemon juice

1 teaspoon vanilla extract
¼ cup sugar
2 large eggs

Topping

5 oz (140g) frozen mixed berries
½ cup strawberry jelly (jam)
¼ cup sugar

1 Preheat oven to 330°F (165°C).

2 For base, combine crumbs, butter and sugar. Line four 4 in (10cm) springform tins with baking paper, then press mixture evenly onto bottoms of tins. Bake for 5 minutes. Cool.

3 For filling, combine cream cheese, juice, vanilla and sugar in an electric mixer. Mix on medium speed until well combined. Add the eggs one at a time, mixing well after each addition. Pour filling over the base.

4 Bake for 25 minutes. Cool before removing from tins.

5 Meanwhile, in a small saucepan over a low heat, combine the berries, jelly and sugar. Simmer gently for 10 minutes, stirring occasionally. Remove from the heat and cool.

6 Once both the cheesecakes and the berries are cool, spoon the berry topping over each cheesecake and serve immediately.

Serves 4 • Preparation 30 minutes • Cooking 40 minutes

ESPRESSO CHEESECAKE

1 cup chocolate graham cracker
  (digestive biscuit) crumbs
1 oz (30g) butter, melted
1 tablespoon sugar
9 oz (250g) bittersweet chocolate,
  chopped
2 lb (1kg) cream cheese
1 cup sugar
1 cup sour cream
2 large eggs, plus 2 egg yolks

¼ cup freshly brewed espresso coffee
1 teaspoon vanilla extract
1 tablespoon freshly ground coffee

Ganache
1 cup heavy (double) cream
5¼ oz (150g) bittersweet chocolate,
  chopped
1 tablespoon instant espresso coffee,
  dissolved in 2 tablespoons water

1 Preheat oven to 360°F (180°C). Mix together crumbs, butter and sugar in a bowl, then press into the bottom of a 8½ in (22cm) springform tin. Place in refrigerator while you make the filling.

2 Melt chocolate in the top of a double boiler and set aside to cool. With an electric mixer, cream the cream cheese and sugar until light and fluffy, then add sour cream; mix, ensuring you scrape down the side of the bowl.

3 Add eggs and egg yolks until well mixed, then add espresso, vanilla, ground coffee and melted chocolate until well blended. Scrape down the sides of the bowl and blend mixture another minute to ensure it's well mixed.

4 Pour mixture into prepared crust, and place springform tin into a water bath. Bake for 45 minutes. Turn off oven and allow to cool slowly for at least 1 hour before removing.

5 While cheesecake is cooling, make the ganache. In a small saucepan, bring cream to the boil, pour the chopped chocolate over and let stand for 1 minute. Stir to dissolve and then stir espresso into the chocolate mixture.

6 Let cool to room temperature. Pour onto top of cooled cheesecake. Refrigerate for a couple of hours to allow to set.

Serves 12 • Preparation 45 minutes • Cooking 60 minutes

BAKED CHEESECAKE

Base
2 oz (60g) butter
1 tablespoon honey
4 oz (125g) crushed wheat-free cookie
  crumbs or gluten-free corn cereal
½ cup shredded coconut

Filling
1 lb (500g) firm cream cheese
8 oz (250g) soft cream or ricotta
  cheese

1 tablespoon sour cream
1 cup superfine (caster) sugar
2 eggs
2 tablespoons vanilla essence
sprinkle of nutmeg

Topping
1 cup cream
whipped and grated chocolate or fresh
  fruit

1 Preheat oven to 300°F (150°C).

2 To make the base, melt the butter and honey over a low heat and mix with
  the cereal or crumbs. You may need a little hot water if the cereal is dry.
  Combine with the coconut and press into a removable base cake tin.

3 To make the filling, beat the cheeses and sour cream with the superfine
  sugar until creamy. Add the eggs one at a time and whip on high speed. Add
  the vanilla essence to the mixture and pour into the uncooked crumb case.
  Sprinkle with nutmeg and place into the centre of the oven for 1 hour. Turn
  the heat off and leave in the oven for an additional hour to set.

4 Serve cold, with whipped cream, fresh fruit or grated chocolate.

Serves 4 • Preparation 35 minutes • Cooking 1 hour

GUAVA STRAWBERRY CHEESECAKE

Base
¾ cup all-purpose (plain) flour
2 oz (60g) butter
1 egg yolk
3 tablespoons lemon juice

Filling
9 oz (250g) ricotta
½ cup natural yogurt
2 eggs
2 tablespoons lemon juice
¼ cup sugar
9 oz (250g) strawberries, sliced
3½ oz (100g) guava jelly (jam)

1 Sift the flour into a bowl. Rub in the butter in. Add the egg yolk and lemon juice, with a little cold water if required, to make a soft dough. Knead on a lightly floured surface until smooth, then press the dough evenly over the bottom of a 9 in (23cm) springform tin. Rest in refrigerator for 30 minutes.

2 Preheat oven to 375°F (190°C). Cover loosely with baking paper and dried beans. Bake blind for 10 minutes, remove the paper and beans and return to the oven for 5 minutes more. Cool.

3 For the filling, reduce the oven temperature to 360°F (180°C). Beat the ricotta, yogurt, eggs, lemon juice and sugar in a bowl until smooth. Pour over the pastry base. Bake for 30 minutes or until set, then cool.

4 Purée a little less than half the strawberries in a blender or food processor with the guava jelly. Spread over the cheesecake. Place in the refrigerator for 1 hour. Decorate with the remaining strawberries to serve.

Serves 12 • Preparation 45 minutes • Cooking 60 minutes

BLACK CHERRY CHEESECAKE

Base
2 oz (60g) graham crackers (digestive biscuits), finely crushed
1 tablespoon sugar
¼ teaspoon ground cinnamon
¼ teaspoon ground nutmeg

Filling
5 eggs
1 cup sugar

1 lb (500g) cream cheese, softened
1 cup sour cream
2 tablespoons all-purpose (plain) flour
1 teaspoon vanilla extract

Glaze
15 oz (425g) canned black cherries
5¼ oz (150g) black cherry jelly (jam)
½ cup sugar

1 Preheat oven to 275°F (135°C).

2 Butter a 9 in (23cm) springform tin and line with baking paper.

3 Combine crumbs, sugar, cinnamon and nutmeg and sprinkle evenly over tin. Set aside.

4 For the filling, separate eggs and beat yolks until they are a lemon shade, then gradually add sugar. Cut cream cheese into tiny chunks, beat until smooth, then slowly add egg yolk mixture. Beat until smooth, then add sour cream, flour and vanilla. Beat again until smooth. Beat egg whites until stiff but not dry. Gently fold egg whites into cream cheese mixture. Pour into prepared tin and bake for 1 hour 10 minutes.

5 Turn off heat and leave in oven for 1 hour longer without opening oven door.

6 For the glaze, drain the cherries and place ½ cup of the liquid with the jelly and sugar in a saucepan, bring to the boil and reduce by half. Add the cherries and simmer for a further 3 minutes. Cool and pour over the cooled cheesecake.

Serves 12 • Preparation 40 minutes • Cooking 1 hour 10 minutes

BIRTHDAY CHEESECAKE

7 oz (200g) plain chocolate cookies, crushed
3½ oz (100g) butter, melted
1 lb 2 oz (550g) cottage cheese
¾ cup superfine (caster) sugar
½ tablespoon vanilla extract
1 tablespoon malt powder
¼ cup milk
1 cup cream
1 tablespoon gelatin
1 teaspoon cochineal (pink food dye)
1 teaspoon cocoa powder
2 egg whites

1 Combine cookie crumbs and butter and press into the base of a 8½ in (22cm) springform tin. Soften cheese and beat in sugar. Add vanilla, malt powder and milk, then fold in the cream.

2 Dissolve gelatin in 2 tablespoons hot water and add to cheese mixture. Divide mixture into three and place in separate bowls.

3 To one bowl, add the cochineal, and to another, add the cocoa. Beat egg whites until stiff and fold one-third into each bowl. Pour pink layer onto crust base and smooth.

4 Gently spoon plain layer on top of the pink layer and smooth. Finally, top with chocolate layer and smooth.

5 Refrigerate until firm. Decorate with whipped cream and chocolate buttons to serve.

Serves 12 • Preparation 40 minutes

MINI RICOTTA CHEESECAKE

9 oz (250g) smooth ricotta
1 cup fruit yogurt
½ cup puréed fruit
1 tablespoon gelatin
8 plain, round, vanilla cookies
sliced fruit to decorate

1 Beat ricotta and yogurt together until smooth. Add fruit and mix well.
2 Dissolve gelatin in 2 tablespoons hot water, then add to ricotta mixture and mix thoroughly. Pour into 8 half-cup Jell-O® moulds.
3 Lightly press a cookie on top of each and refrigerate until set. Carefully unmould, then decorate with fresh fruit.

Note: Any fruit yogurt or purée of fruit may be used.

Serves 8 • Preparation 25 minutes

SUMMER CHEESECAKE

1 cup sweet cookie crumbs
2 oz (60g) butter, melted
1 tablespoon gelatin
1 lb (500g) cream cheese, softened
14 oz (400g) canned condensed milk
½ cup lemon juice
½ cup apricot purée
1 tablespoon Cointreau
14 oz (400g) canned apricot halves
2 tablespoons toasted flaked almonds

1 Combine cookie crumbs and butter, press into base of an 8 in (20cm) springform tin and chill.

2 Heat gelatin with ¼ cup water until melted and clear.

3 Beat cream cheese until smooth, add gelatin mixture, condensed milk, lemon juice, apricot purée and Cointreau. Mix well until smooth. Pour into crumb base and chill for 2–3 hours.

4 Top with apricot halves and press toasted almond flakes onto sides before serving.

Serves 10 • Preparation 20 minutes

CAPPUCCINO CHEESECAKE

1¼ cups chocolate wafers, crushed
¼ teaspoon ground cinnamon
1 cup light cream cheese
1 cup sugar
1 cup unsweetened cocoa powder
2 eggs
2½ cups sour cream
2 tablespoon coffee liqueur
1 teaspoon vanilla extract
2 tablespoons cocoa powder, for dusting

1 Preheat oven to 365°F (185°C). Stir together wafer crumbs and cinnamon. Pat into bottom of 8½ in (22cm) springform tin.

2 Beat cream cheese until light and fluffy. Beat in sugar and cocoa powder, then beat in eggs. Stir in 2 cups sour cream, the coffee liqueur and vanilla. Turn into prepared pan and bake for 30 minutes or until set.

3 Spread remaining sour cream evenly over top. Return to oven for 1 minute. Cool to room temperature, then chill thoroughly, covered. Remove from springform tin. Just before serving, dust with extra cocoa powder.

Serves 8 • Preparation 10 minutes • Cooking 35 minutes

ICE CREAM CHEESECAKE

2 cups plain, sweet cookie crumbs
6 oz (170g) butter, melted
13 oz (375g) cream cheese, softened
¾ cup superfine (caster) sugar
6 oz (200g) fresh or frozen berries
4 cups vanilla ice cream

1 Combine cookie crumbs and butter in a bowl and mix well. Press mixture over base and sides of an 8 in (20cm) springform tin and refrigerate until firm.

2 Beat cheese and sugar together in a bowl until the mixture is smooth. Blend or process berries until smooth, then add to the cheese mixture.

3 Chop up the ice cream, add to the cheese mixture and beat until smooth.

4 Pour filling into crust and freeze for several hours or until firm. Decorate with whipped cream and fresh berries.

Serves 8–10 • Preparation 30 minutes

ORANGE AND LIME CHEESECAKE

1 cup plain, sweet cookies, crushed
2 oz (60g) butter, melted
shredded coconut, toasted

Orange and lime filling
9 oz (250g) cream cheese, softened
2 tablespoons brown sugar
1½ teaspoons finely grated orange zest
1½ teaspoons finely grated lime zest
3 teaspoons orange juice
3 teaspoons lime juice
1 egg, lightly beaten
½ cup sweetened condensed milk
2 tablespoons heavy (double) cream, whipped

1 Preheat oven to 360°F (180°C).

2 Place the cookie crumbs and butter in a bowl and mix to combine. Press the cookie mixture over the base and up the sides of a well-buttered 9 in (23cm) flan tin with a removable base. Bake for 5–8 minutes, then cool.

3 To make the orange and lime filling, place the cream cheese, sugar, orange and lime zests and juices in a bowl and beat until creamy. Beat in the egg, then mix in the condensed milk and fold in the cream.

4 Spoon the filling into the prepared cookie case and bake for 25–30 minutes or until just firm. Turn the oven off and cool the cheesecake in the oven with the door ajar. Chill before serving. Serve decorated with the toasted coconut.

Serves 8 • Preparation 30 minutes • Cooking 40 minutes

CARAMEL CHEESECAKE

Base
5½ oz (150g) graham crackers
 (digestive biscuits), finely crushed
2 oz (60g) butter, melted

Filling
¼ cup evaporated milk
14 oz (400g) canned caramel

1 cup pecans, chopped
1 lb (500g) cream cheese
½ cup sugar
2 eggs
1 teaspoon vanilla extract
¾ cup chocolate chips, melted

1 Preheat oven to 360°F (180°C).

2 To make the base, combine crushed graham cracker crumbs and melted butter. Press mixture evenly into a 9 in (23cm) springform tin. Bake for 8 minutes. Remove from oven and allow to cool.

3 To make the filling, combine milk and caramel in a heavy-based saucepan. Cook over low heat until melted, stirring often. Pour over crushed cracker base. Sprinkle pecans evenly over caramel layer and set aside.

4 Beat cream cheese at high speed with electric mixer until light and fluffy. Gradually add sugar, mixing well. Add eggs one at a time, beating well after each addition. Stir in vanilla and melted chocolate, beat until blended. Pour over pecan layer.

5 Bake for 30 minutes. Remove from oven and run knife around edge of tin to release sides. Cool to room temperature. Cover and chill for 8 hours.

6 Decorate with a chopped flaky chocolate bar and chopped jersey caramels. Serve with whipped cream.

Makes 12 slices • Preparation 30 minutes, plus standing time • Cooking 40 minutes

RAISIN AND BOURBON CHEESECAKE

Base
4 tablespoons finely crushed graham crackers (digestive biscuits)
1 oz (30g) butter, melted
¼ cup sugar

Filling
1½ cups raisins
¼ cup bourbon
1 lb (500g) cream cheese, softened
¼ cup sugar
1 tablespoon lemon juice
zest of ½ lemon
2 large eggs

1 Preheat oven to 330°F (165°C).

2 Soak the raisins in the bourbon for at least 2 hours.

3 To make the base, combine crumbs, butter and sugar. Line four 4 in (10cm) springform tins with baking paper, then press mixture evenly onto bottoms of tins. Bake for 5 minutes.

4 To make the filling, combine cream cheese, sugar, juice and zest in an electric mixer; mix on medium speed until well blended. Add eggs one at a time, mixing thoroughly between additions. Roughly chop 1 cup of the soaked raisins and add to the filling, then divide filling evenly between tins.

5 Bake for 25 minutes. Cool before removing from tins, then chill.

6 Let stand at room temperature for minimum of 40 minutes. Decorate with the remaining raisins and serve with whipped cream.

Serves 4 • Preparation 30 minutes, plus standing time • Cooking 30 minutes

HAZELNUT RASPBERRY CHEESECAKE

Base
7 oz (200g) biscotti, finely crushed
2 oz (60g) butter, melted

Filling
2 lb (1kg) cream cheese, softened
1¼ cups sugar
3 large eggs
1 cup sour cream
1 teaspoon vanilla extract
6 oz (170g) hazelnut spread
⅓ cup raspberry conserve

1 Preheat oven to 330°F (165°C).

2 To make the base, combine biscotti crumbs and butter, press onto bottom of a 9 in (23cm) springform tin.

3 To make the filling, combine three-quarters of the cream cheese with the sugar in an electric mixer and mix on medium speed until well blended. Add eggs one at a time, beating well after each addition. Blend in sour cream and vanilla, then pour over base.

4 Combine remaining cream cheese and the hazelnut spread in the electric mixer, mix on medium speed until well blended. Add raspberry conserve, mix well.

5 Drop heaped tablespoonfuls of hazelnut mixture into plain cream cheese filling – do not swirl.

6 Bake for 1 hour and 25 minutes. Loosen cake from rim of tin, cool before removing. Serve with fresh raspberries.

Makes 12 slices • Preparation 30 minutes • Cooking 1 hour 25 minutes

NUTTY COFFEE CHEESECAKE

Base
1½ cups finely chopped nuts, such as almonds and walnuts
2 tablespoons sugar
1¾ oz (50g) butter, melted

Filling
2 lb (1kg) cream cheese, at room temperature
1 cup sugar
3 tablespoons all-purpose (plain) flour
4 large eggs
1 cup sour cream
1 tablespoon instant coffee powder
¼ teaspoon ground cinnamon
whipped cream and coffee beans to decorate

1 Preheat oven to 320°F (160°C).
2 Combine nuts, sugar and butter, press onto bottom of 9 in (23cm) springform tin. Bake for 10 minutes, remove from oven and allow to cool. Increase oven temperature to 450°F (230°C).
3 Combine cream cheese, sugar and flour in an electric mixer, mix on medium speed until well blended. Add eggs, one at a time, mixing well after each addition. Blend in sour cream.
4 Dissolve coffee and cinnamon in ¼ cup boiling water. Cool, then gradually add to cream cheese mixture, mixing until well blended. Pour over base.
5 Bake for 10 minutes. Reduce oven temperature to 250°F (120°C) and continue baking for 1 hour.
6 Loosen cake from rim, allow to cool before removing. Chill. Serve topped with whipped cream and coffee beans.

Makes 12 slices • Preparation 30 minutes • Cooking 1 hour 20 minutes

CHOC PASSION CHEESECAKE

Base
120g graham crackers (digestive biscuits), finely crushed
3 tablespoons sugar
1¾ oz (50g) butter, melted

Filling
2 oz (60g) cooking chocolate
1½ oz (40g) butter
1 lb (500g) cream cheese, at room temperature
1¼ cups sugar
5 large eggs
1⅓ cups shredded coconut

Topping
1 cup sour cream
2 tablespoons sugar
2 tablespoons passionfruit liqueur
1 teaspoon instant coffee powder

1 Preheat oven to 350°F (175°C).
2 Combine crumbs, sugar and butter, press onto bottom of 9 in (23cm) springform tin. Bake for 10 minutes.
3 Melt chocolate and butter over low heat, stirring until smooth.
4 Combine cream cheese and sugar in an electric mixer, mix on medium speed until well blended. Add eggs one at a time, mixing well after each addition. Blend in chocolate mixture and coconut, pour over base.
5 Bake for 60 minutes or until set.
6 Combine sour cream, sugar, liqueur and coffee, spread over cheesecake.
7 Reduce heat to 300°F (150°C) and bake for 5 minutes.
8 Loosen cake from rim of tin, cool before removing. Chill and serve dusted with cocoa powder.

Makes 12 slices • Preparation 30 minutes • Cooking 1 hour 15 minutes

Tarts
AND FLANS

Elegant concoctions for lovely ladies
and hungry gents

MINI STRAWBERRY CUSTARD TART

12 frozen mini shortcrust pastry cases
2 egg yolks
2 tablespoons superfine (caster) sugar
$1/3$ cup heavy (double) cream
$1\frac{1}{2}$ tablespoons strawberry jelly (jam)
6 small strawberries, hulled and halved
1 tablespoon confectioner's (icing) sugar

1 Preheat the oven to 320°F (160°C). Place the frozen tart cases on an oven tray and bake for 10 minutes. Remove from the oven and set aside to cool slightly.

2 Meanwhile, whisk the egg yolks and sugar by hand until the sugar dissolves, then stir in the cream.

3 Spread the base of each tart case with ½ teaspoon of strawberry jelly. Spoon the egg mixture evenly into each tart case, then bake for 10–12 minutes until the custard is set. When set, take from the oven and place a strawberry half, cut-side down, onto each tart.

4 Leave to cool for 15 minutes, then remove the foil cases. Place on a platter and dust with confectioner's sugar to serve.

Makes 12 • Preparation 30 minutes • Cooking 20 minutes

CHOCOLATE TART

7 oz (200g) plain sweet cookies, crushed
3½ oz (100g) butter, melted
150g milk chocolate, roughly chopped
5 oz (150g) semisweet (dark) chocolate, roughly chopped
2 tablespoons confectioner's (icing) sugar, sifted
1¼ cups heavy (double) cream, whipped
1¾oz (50g) white chocolate

1 Lightly grease the base of a 8 in (20cm) springform tin.

2 Combine crushed cookies and butter in a bowl. Press mixture into base of tin. Chill for 30 minutes until set.

3 Combine milk and semisweet chocolate in a microwave-safe bowl. Melt on medium (50%) power for 1 minute. Stir and return to oven for 30 seconds. Continue cooking in this way until melted and smooth. Mix in confectioner's sugar. Set aside to cool slightly.

4 Fold cream through chocolate. Pour over cookie base. Smooth top and chill for 5 hours or overnight, until set. Melt white chocolate, pipe or drizzle over tart and serve.

Serves 8 • Preparation 35 minutes • Cooking 3 minutes

Tarts and flans   249

PEAR AND FIG FLAN

Hazelnut pastry
2 cups flour, sifted
1½ oz (45g) finely chopped hazelnuts
1 teaspoon ground mixed spice
7 oz (200g) butter, chilled and cut into small cubes
1 egg yolk, lightly beaten with a few drops vanilla extract

Pear and fig filling
4 pears, peeled, cored and quartered
3 oz (90g) butter
4 oz (125g) dried figs, chopped
½ cup brown sugar
½ cup corn (golden) syrup
½ teaspoon vanilla extract
½ cup all-purpose (plain) flour
1 egg, lightly beaten

1 Preheat oven to 430°F (220°C). To make pastry, place flour, hazelnuts and mixed spice in a bowl then, using fingertips, rub in butter until mixture resembles fine breadcrumbs. Using a metal spatula or round-ended knife, mix in egg yolk mixture and enough chilled water (3–4 tablespoons) to form a soft dough. Turn dough onto a lightly floured surface and knead gently until smooth. Wrap dough in cling wrap and chill for 30 minutes.

2 On a lightly floured surface, roll out pastry and use it to line a lightly buttered, deep 9 in (23cm) flan tin. Chill for 15 minutes. Line pastry case with baking paper, fill with uncooked rice and bake for 10 minutes. Remove rice and paper and cook for 10 minutes more.

3 To make filling, cut each pear quarter into four slices. Melt half the butter in a frying pan over a medium heat, add pears and cook for 4–5 minutes. Arrange pear slices in pastry case, then scatter with figs.

4 Place remaining butter, sugar, corn syrup, ½ cup water and the vanilla in a saucepan and cook over a medium heat until sugar dissolves. Bring to the boil and simmer for 2 minutes.

5 Remove pan from heat and set aside to cool for 15 minutes, then beat in flour and egg. Pour mixture over pears and figs and bake at 360°F (180°C) for 50–55 minutes or until filling is firm.

Serves 8 • Preparation 1 hour • Cooking 1½ hours

RHUBARB AND APPLE TART

Pastry
1 cup all-purpose (plain) flour, sifted
2 teaspoons confectioner's (icing) sugar, sifted
3 oz (90g) butter, cubed

Rhubarb and apple filling
6 stalks rhubarb, chopped

2 tablespoons sugar
1 oz (30g) butter
3 green apples, cored, peeled, sliced
4 oz (125g) cream cheese
1/3 cup sugar
1 teaspoon vanilla extract
1 egg

1 Preheat oven to 400°F (200°C). To make pastry, place flour and confectioner's sugar in a bowl and rub in butter, using your fingertips, until mixture resembles coarse breadcrumbs. Add 4 teaspoons iced water and knead to a smooth dough. Wrap in cling wrap and refrigerate for 30 minutes.

2 Roll out pastry on a lightly floured surface and line a buttered 9 in (23cm) fluted flan tin with removable base. Line pastry case with non-stick baking paper and weigh down with uncooked rice. Bake for 15 minutes. Remove rice and paper and cook for 5 minutes longer.

3 To make filling, poach rhubarb until tender. Drain well, stir in sugar and set aside to cool. Melt butter in a frying pan and cook apples for 3–4 minutes. Remove apples from pan and set aside to cool.

4 Place cream cheese, sugar, vanilla extract and egg in a bowl and beat until smooth. Spoon rhubarb into pastry case, then top with cream cheese mixture and arrange apple slices attractively on top. Reduce oven to 360°F (180°C) and cook for 40–45 minutes or until filling is firm.

Serves 10 • Preparation 45 minutes • Cooking 1 hour 15 minutes

RASPBERRY AND HAZELNUT TARTS

Pastry
1 cup flour, sifted
2 tablespoons confectioner's (icing) sugar
2 tablespoons hazelnuts, ground
2½ oz (80g) unsalted butter, chopped
1 egg, lightly beaten

Cream filling
13 oz (375g) cream cheese
2 tablespoons superfine (caster) sugar
¼ cup heavy (double) cream

Raspberry topping
12 oz (350g) raspberries
⅓ cup raspberry jelly (jam), warmed and sieved

1 To make pastry, place flour, confectioner's sugar and hazelnuts in a bowl and mix to combine. Rub in butter, using fingertips, until mixture resembles fine breadcrumbs. Add egg and mix to form a soft dough. Wrap in cling wrap and refrigerate for 1 hour.

2 Preheat oven to 400°F (200°C). Knead pastry lightly, then roll out to ⅛ in (3mm) thick and line six lightly buttered 3 in (7½cm) flan tins with the pastry. Line pastry cases with baking paper, weigh down with uncooked rice and bake for 10 minutes. Remove paper and rice and bake for 15 minutes longer or until golden. Set aside to cool.

3 To make filling, place cream cheese and sugar in a bowl and beat until smooth. Beat cream until soft peaks form then fold into cream cheese mixture. Cover and chill for 20 minutes.

4 To assemble, spoon filling into pastry cases and smooth tops. Arrange raspberries over top of tarts, then brush warm jelly over raspberries and refrigerate for a few minutes to set glaze.

Serves 6 • Preparation 40 minutes • Cooking 25 minutes

FRESH FRUIT TARTLETS

Sweet almond pastry
¼ cup all-purpose (plain) flour
¾ cups self-rising (self-raising) flour
⅓ cup cornstarch (cornflour)
⅓ cup ground almonds
¼ cup confectioner's (icing) sugar
5 oz (150g) butter
1 egg yolk

Filling
3½ oz (100g) ricotta cheese
¼ cup sugar

⅓ cup cream pure cream
¼ cup milk mixed with 1 tablespoon
  of arrowroot
½ cup cooked white short-grain rice
  or semolina
fruit for decorating (for example,
  blueberries, strawberries, peaches,
  mangoes)
¼ cup apple and blackcurrant jelly
  (jam), warmed

1 Preheat oven to 375°F (190°C). To make the pastry, combine flours, almonds and sugar in a bowl. Rub in butter until mixture resembles fine breadcrumbs. Stir in egg and enough iced water (about ¼ cup) to make ingredients just come together. Knead on a floured surface until smooth. Wrap in cling wrap. Refrigerate for at least 30 minutes.

2 Roll out pastry to ⅛ in (3mm) thick. Using a 3 in (7½cm) round fluted cutter, cut out 24 rounds. Gently ease pastry into buttered muffin or patty pans. Prick all over with a fork. Line with foil or baking paper. Weigh down with uncooked rice and bake for 10 minutes. Remove rice and foil. Bake for a further 5–6 minutes or until golden, then cool.

3 Mix ricotta cheese, sugar and cream until light and smooth. Combine ricotta mixture and milk mixture in a saucepan. Cook, stirring, over medium heat for 5–10 minutes or until mixture starts to thicken. Cool. Divide mixture between pastry cases. Top with fruit. Brush with warmed jelly. Chill until ready to serve.

Makes 24 • Preparation 50 minutes • Cooking 25 minutes

PRINCESS CUSTARD TART

Pastry
1½ cups all-purpose (plain) flour
1 teaspoon baking powder
3 oz (90g) butter
pinch of salt
¼ cup sugar
¼ cup raspberry jelly (jam)

Custard
2 teaspoons sugar
1 teaspoon all-purpose (plain) flour
2 egg yolks
1 cup milk

Meringue
3 egg whites
6 tablespoons sugar

1   Preheat oven to 400°F (200°C). Sift flour and baking powder into butter, salt and sugar and mix with 2 tablespoons cold water to make a firm dough. Roll out pastry to about ¼ in (6mm) and line the base and sides of a greased 8 in (20cm) springform tin with the pastry.

2   Make custard by mixing sugar, flour, egg yolks and milk together. Fill the pastry case with the custard mixture.

3   Bake for 25 minutes. While baking, make meringue by beating egg whites with 4 tablespoons sugar.

4   Allow tart to cool then spread thinly with raspberry jelly and pile meringue on top. Reduce heat to 250°F (120°C) and bake until brown.

Serves 8 • Preparation 25 minutes • Cooking 30 minutes

APPLE CUSTARD TART

3 cups all-purpose (plain) flour
1 teaspoon salt
6¼ oz (180g) butter
3 eggs
⅓ cup granulated sugar
1½ cups milk
14 oz (400g) canned pie apples

1 Preheat oven to 360°F (180°C). Combine flour and ½ teaspoon of salt in mixing bowl. Mix in butter until mixture resembles breadcrumbs. Mix in enough hot water to form a dough that sticks together, about 6 tablespoons.

2 Shape dough into a ball. Cut in half. Roll out each half on lightly floured surface until 5mm thick. Cut 12 circles from each half using fluted cookie cutter 3 in (7.5cm) in diameter. Fit pastry circles into greased muffin cups, pressing sides so they reach rims.

3 Beat eggs with whisk or electric mixer. Stir in sugar and the remaining ½ teaspoon salt. Gradually blend in milk.

4 Spoon one tablespoon crushed apples into each pastry case and then spoon custard mixture over apples until each pastry is full.

5 Bake until knife inserted in centre of custards comes out clean, about 30 minutes. Remove tarts from muffin cups. Cool on wire racks.

Makes 24 • Preparation 30 minutes • Cooking 30 minutes

CUSTARD AND DATE TART

1¼ cups all-purpose (plain) flour
¼ cup self-rising (self-raising) flour
¼ cup superfine (caster) sugar
3 oz (90g) butter
1 egg
20 pitted dates
1 teaspoon ground nutmeg

Custard
3 eggs, lightly beaten
1 teaspoon vanilla extract
2 tablespoons superfine (caster) sugar
2 cups milk

1 Preheat oven to 375°F (190°C). Sift flours and sugar into a bowl. Rub in butter. Add egg and enough water to make a dough, about 2 teaspoons.

2 Knead on a floured surface until smooth, then refrigerate for 30 minutes.

3 Roll dough out on a lightly floured surface, and line a 9 in (23cm) pie tin, trimming the edges. Pinch a frill around the edge or decorate as desired.

4 Bake blind for 10 minutes, remove rice or beans and bake for a further 10 minutes. Allow pastry to cool.

5 To make the custard, whisk eggs, vanilla and sugar in a bowl until combined. Heat milk until hot, then quickly whisk into the egg mixture.

6 Place dates around the base of the pastry and pour the custard over the date. Reduce heat to 360°F (180°C) and bake for 15 minutes.

7 Sprinkle custard evenly with nutmeg, and bake for a further 15 minutes or until custard is just set. Allow to cool in the refrigerator until cold.

Serves 6–8 • Preparation 30 minutes • Cooking 30 minutes

APRICOT CUSTARD TART

Pastry
125g butter, chilled and chopped
1½ cups all-purpose (plain) flour
2 tablespoons sugar
3 egg yolks

Custard
2 egg yolks

¼ cup sugar
⅛ cup all-purpose (plain) flour
1 cup milk
2 teaspoons vanilla extract

Topping
14 oz (400g) canned apricots, drained

1 Using fingertips, rub butter into flour until mixture resembles coarse meal. Stir in sugar and egg yolks, press mixture together to form a ball and refrigerate in cling wrap for 30 minutes.

2 Preheat oven to 360°F (180°C). Roll pastry between two sheets of wax paper, making the pastry large enough to cover base and sides of a buttered 8½ in (22cm) fluted tart pan. Trim edges, place sheet of foil into pastry, fill with pie weights or dried beans and bake for 20–25 minutes. Remove foil and beans and bake a further 5 minutes, then allow to cool.

3 To make custard, whisk egg yolks, sugar and flour until thick and pale. Heat milk in saucepan until almost boiling, then slowly dribble hot milk into egg mixture, whisking continuously, until all of milk has been added. Return custard to pot and cook over medium-low heat until custard has thickened and coats the back of a spoon, about 5–7 minutes.

4 Place piece of cling wrap directly onto surface of custard (this prevents a 'skin' from forming) and allow to cool completely.

5 Place most of apricots in the base of the pie shell. Spoon custard over apricots and smooth. Place remaining pieces of fruit attractively over tart. Allow to cool completely before serving.

Serves 6–8 • Preparation 45 minutes • Cooking 35 minutes

PORTUGUESE CUSTARD TART

3 sheets frozen puff pastry, thawed
1½ cups milk
5 tablespoons cornstarch (cornflour)
300g superfine (caster) sugar
½ vanilla bean
9 egg yolks

1 Preheat oven to 375°F (190°C). Lightly grease a 12-cup muffin tin and line bottom and sides of cups with puff pastry.

2 In a saucepan, combine milk, cornstarch, sugar and vanilla bean. Cook, stirring constantly, until mixture thickens.

3 Place egg yolks in a medium bowl. Slowly whisk half of the hot milk mixture into the egg yolks. Gradually add egg yolk mixture back to remaining milk mixture, whisking constantly.

4 Cook, stirring constantly, for 5 minutes or until thickened. Remove vanilla bean.

5 Fill pastry-lined muffin cups with egg mixture and bake for 25 minutes, or until pastry is golden brown and filling is lightly browned on top.

Makes 12 • Preparation 30 minutes • Cooking 30 minutes

TRADITIONAL CUSTARD TART

5¼ oz (150g) shortcrust pastry
3 large eggs
¼ cup sugar
1¼ cups milk
2 teaspoons freshly ground nutmeg

1 Preheat the oven to 400°F (200°C). Roll out the pastry and use it to line a 2½ x 7 in (6 x 18cm) springform tin. Prick it all over with a fork and bake blind for 10–15 minutes.

2 Beat the eggs lightly with the sugar. Heat the milk until it begins to steam, then add the egg mixture to it, whisking everything together.

3 Increase the heat to 430°F (220°C). Pour the mixture into the pastry case, sprinkle with ground nutmeg and bake in the centre of the oven for 10 minutes. Turn down the heat to 360°F (180°C) and bake for a further 20–25 minutes until the custard is just set. Remember, it will become firmer as it cools down.

Serves 6 • Preparation 20 minutes • Cooking 50 minutes

LEMON AND RASPBERRY TART

9 in (23cm) sweet flan case, frozen
5¼ oz (150g) fresh raspberries
4 eggs
⅔ cup superfine (caster) sugar
zest of 2 lemons
½ cup heavy (double) cream
1 tablespoon confectioner's (icing) sugar

1 Preheat oven to 360°F (180°C). Place frozen pastry case on an oven tray – do not remove from the foil tin provided. Scatter the raspberries in the base of the flan case.

2 Beat together the eggs, superfine sugar, lemon zest and cream. Strain mixture through a fine sieve and pour over the raspberries. Bake for 30 minutes or until just set.

3 Allow to cool to room temperature, then dust with the confectioner's sugar. Serve with ice cream and raspberries.

Note: If using frozen berries, make sure they are thawed – this is important as frozen berries retain excess water which, if it goes into the custard, will increase the volume of liquid and the recipe will not work.

Serves 4–6 • Preparation 25 minutes • Cooking 30 minutes

BERRY TARTS

1 sheet puff pastry, thawed
3 cups fresh berries
1½ tablespoons superfine (caster) or brown sugar
1 tablespoon milk

1 Preheat oven to 400°F (200°C) and line an oven tray with baking paper. Cut pastry into quarters and place on the prepared oven tray.

2 In a small saucepan over a medium-low heat, cook the berries with the sugar for 2 minutes until soft. Strain through a sieve and reserve the liquid. Divide mixture evenly between pastry squares, then roll edges of pastry in to form a 4 in (10cm) round shape. Brush pastry edges with milk and scatter with a little extra sugar.

3 Bake for 15 minutes or until crisp and golden brown. Use reserved liquid to decorate the serving plate by pouring a thin circle around the edge of each plate.

4 Serve with vanilla yogurt or vanilla ice cream.

Serves 4 • Preparation 15 minutes • Cooking 15 minutes

CHOCOLATE PEAR DELIGHTS

3 sheets puff pastry, thawed
1 cup milk chocolate buttons, melted
1¾ lb (825g) canned pear halves, drained and
  sliced ¼ in (5mm) thick
1/3 cup almond meal

1 Preheat oven to 400°F (200°C) and line 2 oven trays with baking paper. Using a 5½ in (14cm) plate as a stencil, cut out 2 rounds from each pastry sheet, making a total of 6 rounds. Pierce each pastry round all over with a fork, leaving a ½ in (1cm) border, then place on the prepared oven trays.

2 Spread each round with 1–2 tablespoons of melted chocolate, leaving a ½ in (1cm) border. Add the sliced pear halves and almond meal to a bowl and gently mix to combine. Divide the pear slices evenly between the pastry rounds and arrange decoratively. Bake for 12–15 minutes.

3 Serve with ice cream, and if you like, drizzle with melted chocolate.

Note: One of the easiest ways to melt chocolate is to place chopped chocolate in a safe container and microwave on high in 30-second bursts, stirring a little each time, until melted.

Serves 6 • Preparation 10 minutes • Cooking 15 minutes

STRAWBERRY TARTLETS

1 cup all-purpose (plain) flour
1 tablespoon superfine (caster) sugar, plus extra to dust
3½ oz (100g) unsalted butter, softened
finely grated zest of 1 small lemon, plus 1 teaspoon juice
½ cup heavy (double) cream
9 oz (250g) strawberries, halved
4 tablespoons raspberry or redcurrant jelly (jam)

1 Preheat the oven to 375°F (190°C). Sift the flour and sugar into a bowl. Rub in the butter and the lemon juice, and knead lightly until the mixture forms a smooth dough. Cover with cling wrap and refrigerate for 15 minutes.

2 Roll the dough out thinly on a lightly floured surface, divide it into 4 and use it to line four 3 in (7.5cm) loose-bottomed tartlet tins. Line with baking paper and baking beans (or uncooked rice) and bake for 15 minutes. Remove the paper and beans and cook for another 3–5 minutes, until the pastry is golden. Leave to cool for 15 minutes, then remove from the tins.

3 Whip the cream with the lemon zest until it forms soft peaks. Spoon into the cases and top with the strawberries. Melt the selected jelly over a gentle heat with 1 tablespoon of water, then press through a sieve and cool slightly. Spoon over the strawberries, then dust with confectioner's sugar and serve.

Serves 4 • Preparation 30 minutes • Cooking 20 minutes

APPLE JAM TARTS

8 oz (250g) shortcrust pastry
1 lb (500g) apples, peeled and cored
juice and zest of 1 lemon
60g sugar
1 oz (30g) butter
2 eggs, lightly beaten
$^{1}/_{3}$ cup blackberry jelly (jam)

1 Preheat oven to 400°F (200°C). Line 8 patty tins with the pastry, prick with a fork and cook for about 10–15 minutes, until browned. Cook the apples with water and cook for 15 minutes.

2 When cooked, rub through a sieve, return to the saucepan and add lemon zest, juice, sugar, butter and eggs. Allow to cook over a low heat until the mixture thickens slightly.

3 Place a teaspoon or two of the jelly in the bottom of each pastry case and then fill the cases with the apple mixture and return to oven to set. Serve sprinkled with sifted confectioner's sugar.

Serves 8 • Preparation 20 minutes • Cooking 15 minutes

ASSORTED JAM TARTS

2²/₃ cups all-purpose (plain) flour
6 oz (200g), chilled and diced
1¾ (50g) superfine (caster) sugar
2 egg yolks
zest of 1 orange
¾ cup jelly (jam)

1 Process the flour and butter in a food processor or blender until it resembles breadcrumbs. Add the superfine sugar and mix. Add the yolks and orange zest and pulse until it comes together (you might need to add a splash of water). Wrap in cling wrap and chill for 20 minutes.
2 Preheat the oven to 375°F (190°C). Roll out the pastry and stamp out circles big enough to fit two 12-hole mini muffin or tart tins.
3 Bake for 15 minutes, then add small spoonfuls of jelly to each and bake for a further 5 minutes.

Note: You can use any jelly for these tarts, or a combination of different jellies.

Makes 24 • Preparation 30 minutes • Cooking 20 minutes

HOMELAND JAM TARTS

1 sheet shortcrust pastry
1½ cups frozen raspberries
½ cup superfine (caster) sugar
juice of ½ lemon

1 Preheat the oven to 400°F (200°C).

2 Line a baking tray with baking paper, place a ring mould onto the tray. Cut a large round from the pastry and use to line the base and sides of the mould to form a tart case. Trim the excess pastry. Bake blind for 6–8 minutes or until the pastry is light golden.

3 Place the raspberries and sugar in a bowl, add the lemon juice and microwave for 6–8 minutes on high (100%) or until thickened and jelly-like.

4 Remove the mould from the pastry case. Spoon the jelly into the pastry case and allow to cool before serving. Dust with confectioner's sugar and serve with whipped cream.

Serves 6 • Preparation 20 minutes • Cooking 10 minutes

MINIATURE JAM TARTS

120g unsalted butter, softened
180g cream cheese, softened
1 cup brown sugar, firmly packed
1 teaspoon vanilla extract
1 egg
2¼ cups all-purpose (plain) flour, sifted
¾ cup jelly (jam) or preserves
¾ cup pecans, toasted and chopped

1 Combine butter and cream cheese in large mixing bowl. Beat until well mixed. Add brown sugar and beat until the sugar dissolves. Add vanilla and egg, beat again until mixed thoroughly.

2 Gradually add flour and beat until a dough forms. Shape dough into a ball and double wrap in baking paper. Refrigerate at least 2 hours until quite firm.

3 Preheat oven to 360°F (180°C). Divide the dough, pinching off 48 equal pieces. Roll each into a 1 in (2.5cm) ball and press into greased mini-muffin tins. Spoon a teaspoon of jelly into each cup. Sprinkle top of tarts with some of the toasted nuts.

4 Bake for 12–15 minutes until lightly browned. Remove from oven and let stand 15 minutes before attempting to remove from the tins. The dough is quite tender and it will fall apart if you move them too soon. Cool on wire racks. Keep in airtight tins.

Note: Excellent jellies or preserves to use with this recipe include seedless blackberry, orange marmalade, blueberry or fig.

Makes 48 • Preparation 35 minutes • Cooking 15 minutes

GREEK JAM TART

180g butter, at room
temperature, cut into 1 in (2.5cm) pieces
zest of 1 orange or lemon
1/3 cup sugar
2 eggs, at room temperature
3 tablespoons brandy
3 cups all-purpose (plain) flour
3 teaspoons baking soda (bicarbonate of soda)
1½ cups jelly (jam) of your choice

1 Preheat oven to 360°F (180°C). Cream the butter, adding orange or lemon zest, then sugar until light and fluffy. Add eggs one at a time, then brandy, and beat until fully combined. Beat or mix in sifted flour and baking soda until combined. Use hands to form into a smooth dough.

2 Roll out half the dough to fit in the bottom and sides of the ¼ in (5mm) springform tart tin. Spread the jelly evenly over the base of the tart shell.

3 Roll out the remaining dough to about ¼ in (5mm) thickness and cut into strips. For a decorative touch, use a fluted pastry wheel to cut the strips.

4 Place the strips in a latticework (criss-cross) pattern across the top of the tart and bake for about 30 minutes, until golden brown.

Makes 48 • Preparation 35 minutes • Cooking 15 minutes

LEMON MERINGUE TART

Pastry
¾ cup bread (strong plain) flour
2 oz (60g) dairy-free margarine
1 egg yolk
1 tablespoon rice syrup

Lemon filling
¼ cup sugar

juice of 2 lemons
zest of 1 lemon, grated
2 tablespoons tapioca starch
2 egg yolks

Meringue
3 egg whites
½ cup superfine (caster) sugar

1 Preheat the oven to 320°F (160°C). Place the flour, margarine, egg yolk, rice syrup and enough cold water to mix in a food processor. Process until it forms a ball. Tip out and knead lightly, then press the pastry into an ungreased 8 in (20cm) tart ring with a removable base. Bake the pastry for about 20 minutes. Set aside until cool.

2 Place 1 cup water, the sugar, lemon juice and zest in a saucepan, heat until near boiling point, then remove from heat. Mix the tapioca starch with a little cold water and stir into the juice mixture.

3 Return to the heat and stir until the mixture thickens. Whisk the yolks and add them to the mixture, stir well for about 1 minute over the heat.

4 Pour the lemon filling into the cooked pastry case. Beat the egg whites until they are stiff, then gradually add the superfine sugar, beating until it has completely dissolved. Spoon on top of the lemon filling and place in the oven for about 15 minutes.

Serves 4 • Preparation 25 minutes • Cooking 35 minutes

STRAWBERRY CUSTARD FLAN

Pastry
1 cup all-purpose (plain) flour
2 tablespoons superfine (caster) sugar
⅓ cup margarine
1 egg yolk
1 tablespoon iced water

Filling
1 cup milk
3 egg yolks
3 tablespoons sugar
1½ tablespoons all-purpose (plain)
  flour
1 teaspoon vanilla essence
1½ cups strawberries
strawberry jelly (jam), warmed

1 Place the flour, superfine sugar and margarine into the bowl of the food processor. Process until the mixture resembles coarse breadcrumbs.

2 Add the egg yolk and water and mix until the pastry forms a ball around the blade. Remove and knead lightly. Wrap in plastic wrap and refrigerate for 30 minutes.

3 Roll out or press the pastry into a 9 in (23cm) fluted flan tin with a removable base. Prick the base of the pastry with a fork. Bake in a pre-heated oven for 15 minutes or until golden. Cool.

4 For the filling, heat the milk. Beat together the egg yolks, sugar and flour. Gradually pour the hot milk over the egg mixture while mixing well. Return the custard to the saucepan and stir over low heat until the mixture boils and thickens. Add the vanilla essence. Cover with plastic wrap to stop a skin forming and allow to cool.

5 Spread the custard into the baked pie shell. Decorate with the strawberries and brush them with the jelly.

Tip: Make your own superfine sugar by placing a cup of normal crystalline sugar into your blender and blend until finely crushed. If you keep blending, the sugar will become pure confectioner's sugar.

Serves 6–8 • Preparation 45 minutes • Cooking 30 minutes

Brownies
AND SLICES

Slices of heaven

VALENTINE'S BROWNIES

1¼ cups all-purpose (plain) flour
¼ cup sugar
4 oz (125g) butter
14 oz (400ml) condensed milk
¼ cup unsweetened cocoa powder
1 egg
1 teaspoon vanilla extract
½ teaspoon baking powder
9 oz (250g) milk chocolate, broken into chunks
¾ cup chopped nuts

1 Preheat oven to 360°F (180°C). Line a 7 x 11 in (18 x 28cm) baking tin with foil and set aside.

2 Combine 1 cup flour and the sugar, then cut in butter until crumbly. Press onto bottom of pan. Bake for 15 minutes.

3 In another bowl, beat condensed milk, cocoa, egg, remaining ¼ cup flour, vanilla and baking powder. Mix in chocolate pieces and nuts. Spread over prepared crust and bake for 20 minutes or until set.

4 Cool and lift out of pan. Cut with heart-shaped cookie cutter or cut around a cardboard heart template using a knife. Decorate with frosting if desired. Store in an airtight container.

Makes 12 • Preparation 15 minutes • Cooking 20 minutes

CHOCOLATE PANFORTE

1 cup liquid honey
1 cup sugar
9 oz (250g) almonds, toasted and chopped
9 oz (250g) hazelnuts, toasted and chopped
4 oz (125g) glacé apricots, chopped
4 oz (125g) glacé peaches, chopped
3½ oz (100g) candied mixed peel
1¼ cups all-purpose (plain) flour, sifted
¼ cup cocoa powder, sifted
2 teaspoons ground cinnamon
5½ oz (155g) semisweet (dark) chocolate, melted
rice paper

1 Preheat oven to 400°F (200°C). Place honey and sugar in a small saucepan and heat, stirring constantly, over a low heat until sugar dissolves. Bring to the boil, then reduce heat and simmer, stirring constantly, for 5 minutes or until mixture thickens.

2 Place almonds, hazelnuts, apricots, peaches, mixed peel, flour, cocoa powder and cinnamon in a bowl and mix to combine. Stir in honey syrup. Add chocolate and mix well to combine.

3 Line an 7 x 11 in (18 x 28cm) shallow cake tin with rice paper. Pour mixture into tin and bake for 20 minutes. Turn onto a wire rack to cool, then cut into small pieces.

Makes 32 • Preparation 25 minutes • Cooking 25 minutes

SIMPLE BROWNIES

5 oz (150g) butter, softened
½ cup honey, warmed
2 eggs, lightly beaten
1¾ cups self-rising (self-raising) flour, sifted
⅔ cup brown sugar
4 oz (125g) semisweet (dark) chocolate, melted and cooled
confectioner's (icing) sugar, sifted

1 Preheat oven to 360°F (180°C).
2 Place butter, honey, eggs, flour, brown sugar, chocolate and 1 tablespoon of water in a food processor and process until ingredients are combined.
3 Spoon batter into a buttered and lined 9 in (23cm) square cake tin and bake for 30–35 minutes or until cooked when tested with a skewer. Stand cake in tin for 5 minutes before turning onto a wire rack to cool completely.
4 Dust with confectioner's sugar and cut into squares.

Makes 25 • Preparation 15 minutes • Cooking 40 minutes

FRUIT AND NUT BROWNIES

4 oz (125g) semisweet (dark)
  chocolate, chopped
3 oz (90g) butter
2 eggs
1¼ cups superfine (caster) sugar
4 tablespoons walnuts, chopped
3 oz (90g) chocolate-coated raisins
½ cup self-rising (self-raising) flour,
  sifted

Chocolate topping
3 oz (90g) semisweet (dark) chocolate,
  chopped
6 oz (170g) cream cheese
2 tablespoons sugar
1 egg

1 Preheat oven to 320°F (160°C).
2 Place chocolate and butter in a heatproof bowl set over a saucepan of
   simmering water and cook, stirring constantly, until chocolate and butter
   melt and mixture is combined. Remove bowl from heat and set aside to cool
   slightly.
3 Place eggs and superfine sugar in a bowl and beat until foamy. Fold
   chocolate mixture, walnuts, raisins and flour into egg mixture. Spoon batter
   into a buttered and lined 9 in (23cm) springform tin and bake for 40 minutes
   or until top is dry but centre is still moist.
4 To make topping, place chocolate in a heatproof bowl set over a saucepan of
   simmering water and heat until chocolate melts. Remove bowl from heat and
   set aside to cool slightly.
5 Place cream cheese and sugar in a bowl and beat until smooth. Beat in egg,
   then chocolate mixture and continue beating until well combined. Pour
   topping over hot brownies and bake for 15 minutes longer.
6 Allow to cool in tin, then refrigerate for 2 hours before cutting into wedges
   and serving.

Serves 10 • Preparation 30 minutes • Cooking 1 hour 5 minutes

CHOC-MINT BROWNIES

4 oz (125g) butter
7 oz (200g) semisweet (dark) chocolate, grated
2 eggs
¾ cup brown sugar
2 tablespoons cocoa powder
2 tablespoons oil
1 cup all-purpose (plain) flour

Frosting
1 cup confectioner's (icing) sugar
½ oz (15g) butter
3 drops peppermint extract

1 Preheat oven to 320°F (160°C).

2 Melt butter and chocolate in a medium saucepan, stir until combined then cool slightly. Beat eggs and sugar until light and creamy. Beat in cocoa and oil, then beat in flour and cooled chocolate mixture.

3 Pour mixture into a buttered and lined 9 x 9 in (23 x 23cm) square tin. Bake for 40 minutes or until cooked when tested with a skewer. Turn onto wire rack to cool.

4 To make the frosting, sift confectioner's sugar into a heatproof bowl, add butter and peppermint extract and stir over simmering water until smooth. Drizzle or pipe frosting over top of brownies. Cut into squares and serve.

Makes 18–20 brownies • Preparation 20 minutes • Cooking 40 minutes

RASPBERRY YOGURT SLICE

Base
3½ oz (100g) butter
1 cup all-purpose (plain) flour
¼ cup brown sugar
¾ cup rolled oats

Topping
4 oz (125g) cream cheese

¾ cup raspberry yogurt
1 tablespoon honey
1 teaspoon lemon juice
1 teaspoon grated lemon zest
1 tablespoon gelatin
8 oz (250g) frozen raspberries
¼ cup sugar

1 Preheat oven to 360°F (180°C).

2 Blend butter and flour in a food processor with sugar until dough just comes together. Fold through the oats.

3 Press into the base of a buttered and lined 11 x 7 in (28 x 18cm) tin. Bake for about 15–20 minutes or until a skewer comes out clean. Allow to cool.

4 Beat the cream cheese with yogurt and honey, add lemon juice and zest. Sprinkle gelatin over ¼ cup water to soften. Heat three-quarters of the thawed raspberries in a saucepan and add sugar and softened gelatin. Bring to the boil, stirring until sugar and gelatin have thoroughly dissolved. Press through a sieve, cool to egg white consistency. Then stir into the creamed cheese and yogurt mixture with the remaining raspberries.

5 Carefully pour the yogurt mixture over the base and refrigerate overnight. Serve with extra raspberries.

Makes about 15 squares • Preparation 25 minutes, plus standing time
• Cooking 20 minutes

DATE SLICES

Pastry
1 tablespoon gelatin
1 egg
4 oz (125g) butter
2 tablespoons pure confectioner's
 (icing) sugar
2 cups all-purpose (plain) flour

Filing
¾ cup dates

1 tablespoon brown sugar
1 tablespoon water
1 tablespoon corn (golden) syrup
1 teaspoon mixed spice

Lemon frosting
⅔ cup sifted pure confectioner's
 (icing) sugar
1 teaspoon melted butter
lemon juice to mix

1 Preheat the oven to 360°F (180°C). Select a shallow 8 in (20cm) square ungreased cake tin. Soak the gelatin in ¼ cup cold water, then heat gently until dissolved. Cool. Combine all the remaining pastry ingredients in a food processor and process to form a firm pastry.

2 Divide the pastry and press half the mixture into the tin using your fingers. Roll out the other half of the pastry between two sheets of cling wrap for the top of the slice.

3 Warm the dates slightly over a saucepan of hot water. Combine the remainder of the filling ingredients with the softened dates in a food processor and process into a coarse paste.

4 Spread the filling onto the pastry base in the tin and place the rolled out pastry on the top of the date mixture. Prick the top to allow air to escape and give an even appearance when cooked. Brush with water and sprinkle with sugar. Place in the oven and cook for 20 minutes. Cool in the cake tin.

5 To make the lemon frosting, combine all ingredients with 1 tablespoon of boiling water to make a creamy frosting and pour onto the slice. Cut into squares to serve.

Serves 2–4 • Preparation 40 minutes • Cooking 20 minutes

CINNAMON SQUARES

3 oz (90g) dairy-free margarine
2 teaspoons vanilla essence
1 cup all-purpose (plain) flour
¾ cup sugar
1 tablespoon ground cinnamon, sifted
2 egg yolks
2 tablespoons fine rice flour
2 tablespoons olive oil

1 Preheat the oven to 300°F (150°C). Line a baking tray with baking paper.
2 Place all the ingredients except the rice flour and oil in a mixer and blend for a few minutes until the mixture forms a ball. Tip onto a sheet of cling wrap.
3 Knead a few times with the rice flour, then roll out in a thick slab. Cut into shapes with a square cookie cutter.
4 Place on the prepared tray. Brush with olive oil and bake for 10 minutes. Remove from the oven, sprinkle with cinnamon sugar and cool on the tray.

Serves 2–4 • Preparation 12 minutes • Cooking 10 minutes

MELTED CHOCOLATE PECAN BROWNIES

6 oz (200g) dark cooking chocolate
3½ oz (100g) butter
1½ cups white sugar
4 eggs
1 cup all-purpose (plain) flour
½ teaspoon baking powder
1 teaspoon vanilla extract
¼ cup pecans, chopped

1 Preheat oven to 375°F (190°C). Melt chocolate and butter together in a saucepan over a medium heat.
2 Remove from heat, stir in sugar and cool slightly. Add eggs and beat with a wooden spoon to combine. Mix in flour, baking powder and vanilla until smooth. Mix in pecans.
3 Pour into an 8 in (20cm) square cake tin lined with baking paper. Bake for 30–35 minutes or until set. Cut into squares to serve.

Makes 12 • Preparation 20 minutes • Cooking 35 minutes

STICKY CHOCOLATE AND RASPBERRY SLICE

Base
2½ oz (75g) unsalted butter, plus extra for greasing
2½ oz (75g) plain chocolate, broken into chunks
2½ oz (75g) fresh or frozen raspberries, plus extra to decorate
2 medium eggs, separated
¼ cup superfine (caster) sugar
2 tablespoons ground almonds

2 tablespoons cocoa powder, sifted
1½ tablespoons all-purpose (plain) flour
sifted icing sugar to dust
fresh mint to decorate

Raspberry sauce
5 oz (150g) fresh or frozen raspberries
1 tablespoon superfine (caster) sugar (optional)

1 Preheat the oven to 360°F (180°C). Grease the base and sides of a 7 in (18cm) loose-bottomed cake tin and line with baking paper. Melt the butter and chocolate in a bowl set over a saucepan of simmering water, stirring. Cool slightly.

2 Press the raspberries through a sieve. Whisk the egg yolks and sugar until pale and creamy, then mix in the almonds, cocoa, flour, melted chocolate and sieved raspberries.

3 Whisk the egg whites until they form stiff peaks (this is best done with an electric whisk). Fold a little into the chocolate mixture to loosen, then fold in the remainder. Spoon into the tin and cook for 25 minutes or until risen and just firm. Cool for 1 hour.

4 Remove the cake from the tin and dust with the confectioner's sugar.

5 To make the raspberry sauce, sieve the raspberries, then stir in the sugar. Serve with the sauce, and decorate with mint and raspberries.

Serves 6 • Preparation 30 minutes • Cooking 25 minutes

MACADAMIA CARAMEL SQUARES

Base
3 oz (100g) white melting chocolate
4 oz (125g) butter
90g icing sugar
60g macadamia nuts, roasted
  and ground
200g all-purpose (plain) flour

Topping
14 oz (400g) can sweetened
  condensed milk

6 oz (200g) milk chocolate for melting
2 large eggs
2 tablespoons all-purpose (plain) flour
3 oz (90g) shortbread, chopped not
  crushed
6 oz (200g) roasted macadamia nuts
  roughly chopped
2 oz (60g) roasted macadamia nuts
  (extra)

1 Preheat oven to 360°F (180°C). Butter a tin 11 x 7 in (28 x 18cm) then line it with baking paper.

2 Melt the white chocolate, then add it to a mixer with the butter, confectioner's sugar, crushed macadamia nuts and all-purpose flour.

3 Mix on low speed until all the ingredients are combined, then press the mixture into the prepared tin. Bake for 18 minutes, then cool.

4 For the topping, preheat the oven to 320°F (160°C). In a saucepan, heat the condensed milk and milk chocolate together (until the chocolate has melted). Add the eggs, flour, shortbread pieces and chopped macadamia nuts, and mix gently.

5 Pour this mixture over the base, then sprinkle the extra macadamia nuts over. Bake at 320°F (160°C) for 40 minutes. Remove from the oven and cool completely in the refrigerator before slicing.

Makes 8 • Preparation 30 minutes • Cooking 1 hour

CHOCOLATE FLAPJACK

7¾ oz (220g) butter
1 cup raw sugar
¼ cup corn (golden) syrup
3 tablespoons cocoa powder
3½ cups rolled oats
3½ oz (100g) semisweet (dark) chocolate melts

1 Preheat oven to 375°F (190°C). Melt butter, sugar and corn syrup in a saucepan large enough to mix all the ingredients. Mix in cocoa. Remove from heat and mix in rolled oats.

2 Press into a 11 x 7 in (28 x 18cm) shallow tin with a baking-paper-lined base. Bake for 30–35 minutes or until cooked.

3 Cool for 5 minutes before marking flapjacks into squares or fingers.

4 Melt chocolate. Drizzle over flapjacks and leave to set. Cut flapjacks through completely when cold.

Makes 10–12 • Preparation 20 minutes • Cooking 35 minutes

CARAMEL WALNUT PETIT FOURS

1 cup sugar
½ cup brown sugar
2 cups heavy (double) cream
1 cup corn (golden) syrup
2 oz (60g) butter, chopped
½ teaspoon baking soda (bicarbonate of soda)

5 oz (150g) walnuts, chopped
1 tablespoon vanilla extract

Chocolate topping
13 oz (375g) dark or milk chocolate, melted
2 teaspoons vegetable oil

1 Place sugar, brown sugar, cream, corn syrup and butter in a saucepan and heat over a low heat, stirring constantly, until sugar dissolves. As sugar crystals form on sides of pan, brush with a wet pastry brush.

2 Bring syrup to the boil and stir in baking soda. Reduce heat and simmer until syrup reaches the hard ball stage or 250°F (120°C) on a sugar thermometer.

3 Stir in walnuts and vanilla and pour mixture into a buttered and foil-lined 8 in (20cm) square cake tin. Set aside at room temperature for 5 hours or until caramel sets.

4 Remove caramel from tin and cut into ¾ in (2cm) squares.

5 To make topping, combine chocolate and oil. Half-dip caramels in melted chocolate, place on baking paper and leave to set.

Note: For easy removal of the caramel from the tin, allow the foil lining to overhang the tin on two opposite sides to form handles.

Makes 40 • Preparation 35 minutes • Cooking 10 minutes

DOUBLE FUDGE BLONDIE

9 oz (250g) butter, softened
1½ cups sugar
1 teaspoon vanilla extract
4 eggs, lightly beaten
1¾ cups all-purpose (plain) flour
½ teaspoon baking powder
6 oz (185g) white chocolate, melted

Cream cheese filling
9 oz (250g) cream cheese, softened
2 oz (60g) white chocolate, melted
¼ cup maple syrup
1 egg
1 tablespoon all-purpose (plain) flour

1 Preheat oven to 360°F (180°C). To make filling, place cream cheese, chocolate, maple syrup, egg and flour in a bowl and beat until smooth. Set aside.

2 Place butter, sugar and vanilla extract in a bowl and beat until light and fluffy. Gradually beat in eggs.

3 Sift together flour and baking powder over butter mixture. Add chocolate and mix well to combine.

4 Spread half the mixture over the base of a buttered and lined 9 in (23cm) square cake tin. Top with filling, then remaining mixture. Bake for 40 minutes or until firm. Cool in tin, then cut into squares.

Note: These lusciously rich white brownies can double as a dinner party dessert if drizzled with melted white or semisweet chocolate and topped with toasted flaked almonds.

Makes 24 • Preparation 30 minutes • Cooking 40 minutes

Cakes
FOR KIDS

Magic creations for little rascals

SWEET BOMBERS

6 shop-bought jelly (jam) rollettes
12 yellow ice-cream wafers

Butter cream
8 oz (250g) butter
18 oz (500g) confectioner's (icing) sugar, sifted
¼ cup milk
red and blue food dye

1 Taper both ends of the jelly rollettes with a sharp knife to resemble planes.

2 To make the butter cream, beat butter in a small mixing bowl until light and creamy. Add confectioner's sugar and milk and continue to beat until smooth.

3 Dye half the butter cream blue and the other half red.

4 Spread the entire surface of three cakes with red butter cream and three cakes with blue butter cream.

5 Cut wafers in half crossways and curve one end with a sharp knife to resemble wings. Position on each side of cake, pressing into cake. Cut tail fin pieces from remaining wafers, using picture as a guide for the shape. Position as shown in picture.

Makes 6 planes • Preparation 30 minutes

DINOSAUR CAKE

1 slab cake (see note)
green food dye
1 cup shredded coconut
small toy animals, dinosaurs and plants

Butter cream
1¾ cups confectioner's (icing) sugar, sifted
4 oz (125g) butter
⅓ cup milk

1 Trim top of cake so that it is level. Turn upside down on a 9 x 13 in (23 x 33cm) board.

2 To make the butter cream, beat butter in a small mixing bowl until light and creamy. Add confectioner's sugar and milk and continue to beat until smooth.

3 Place the butter cream in a bowl and dye it green. Spread green butter cream over sides and top of cake.

4 Dye the coconut green, sprinkle it over the top of the cake. Decorate the cake with dinosaurs and trees.

Note: You can use a simple cake recipe (e.g. Simple Sponge Cake, page 125) to make the slab cake, baking in a buttered and lined rectangular tin.

Serves 8–10 • Preparation 1 hour

FIRST PRIZE CAKE

8 in (20cm) round cake (see note)
4 x 8 in (10 x 20cm) log cake (see note)

Butter cream
8 oz (250g) butter
18 oz (500g) confectioner's (icing) sugar, sifted
¼ cup milk
blue food dye

1 Cut a triangle out of one end of the log cake. Cut a curve out of the other end, so it fits against the round cake. Fit cakes together and place on board.

2 To make the butter cream, beat butter in a small mixing bowl until light and creamy. Add confectioner's sugar and milk and continue to beat until smooth.

3 Keep a small amount of butter cream plain, dye the rest blue.

4 Cover top and sides with ¾ of the blue butter cream, place the remaining blue butter cream in a piping bag fitted with a star nozzle. Pipe a decorative pattern around the edge of the cake.

5 Spoon the plain butter cream into a piping bag fitted with a plain nozzle, pipe "1st" onto the top of the cake.

Note: You can use a simple cake recipe (e.g. Simple Sponge Cake, page 125) to make the round cake and the log cake, baking in a buttered and lined 8 in (20cm) round tin and a 4 x 8 in (10 x 20cm) log tin.

Serves 8–12 • Preparation 1 hour

CRAZY CLOCK CAKE

1 packet rainbow cake mix

Frosting
Butter cream frosting (page 384)
1 drop red food dye
½ cup sprinkles
M&Ms or similar candy
licorice strips
various candies

1 Make up the cake as directed on the packet. Spoon the mixture into a lightly greased 9 in (23cm) round cake tin. Bake in a pre-heated oven 360°F (180°C) for 30 minutes. Cool in the tin for 10 minutes before turning out on a wire rack to cool completely.

2 Make up the frosting as directed. Place the cake on a serving plate. Spread the frosting over the top and sides of the cake.

3 Place a saucepan lid over the centre of the cake. Decorate the remaining rim of the cake with sprinkles. Remove the lid.

4 Place the M&Ms around the edge of the clock face. Use the candies to make the numbers and cut the licorice for the clock hands.

Serves 8 • Preparation 25 minutes • Cooking 30 minutes

DOTTY BIRTHDAY CAKE

4 x basic cakes (see note), baked in
  two x 8 in (20cm) round tins and two
  x 5 in (12cm) round tins
Sugar paste
Powdered food dye – purple, green
Basic cream frosting (e.g. page 384)
  with lilac food dye

Wooden skewer
Purple ribbon, approximately 3 ft (1m)
  in length
Edible glitter
Small ornamental purple butterfly
Florist's wire
Prestik® or Blu-tac™

1 Bake the cakes according to directions and allow to cool completely.

2 Dye the sugar paste with the powdered food dye and roll out to a thickness
   of ¼ in (4–5 mm). Use the base of a piping bag nozzle to cut out equal-sized
   dots. Use a cutter with an approximate diameter of 1¼ in
   (3.2 cm) to cut out larger dots for the flower. Set all aside to firm up.

3 Trim the cakes if necessary with a serrated knife to level the tops. Sandwich
   the cakes together with frosting before completely coating the larger pair
   with frosting. Place the smaller pair on top of the larger cake, securing with
   a wooden skewer. Coat the top cake with frosting.

4 Arrange the ribbon around the base of each cake, securing with extra
   frosting as necessary. Arrange the larger circles to form a flower in the
   centre of the top cake. Fashion leaves from green sugar paste and arrange
   around the petals as illustrated. Attach the smaller dots, starting just above
   the ribbons, to the sides of the cake in neat rows. Dust the flower petals
   with edible glitter.

5 Attach the butterfly to the wire with a small dab of Prestik®. Insert the wire
   into the cake so that the butterfly hovers over the flower.

**Note: You can use a simple cake recipe (e.g. Simple Sponge Cake, page 125) to make
the round cakes at the dimensions given.**

Serves 20 • Preparation 1 hour

Cakes for kids   335

MY SPECIAL PONY BIRTHDAY CAKE

1 x basic cake (see note), baked in 12½ x 8¾ in (32 x 22cm) tin
Sugar paste
Powdered food dye – yellow
Flower cookie cutters in various sizes
Basic cream frosting (e.g. page 384), dyed pale yellow with food dye
Silver balls
Edible glitter
Plastic toy horses

1 Dye the sugar paste a deeper shade of yellow than the frosting and roll out to ¼ in (4 mm) thick. Use the cutters to make flower shapes. Set them aside to firm up.

2 Bake the cake per the recipe and leave to cool completely.

3 Use a suitable template to trace two half horseshoe shapes on cardboard. Place on the cake, cut out and assemble the cake to form a horseshoe.

4 Join the sections together with frosting.

5 Coat the cake with pale yellow frosting and use the star nozzle to enhance the upper surface.

6 Place the flowers on the cake as illustrated. Add a dab of frosting to the centre of each flower to secure a silver ball.

7 Dust lightly with edible glitter.

8 Arrange the toy horses on the cake.

Note: You can use a simple cake recipe (e.g. Simple Sponge Cake, page 125) to make the cake at the dimensions given.

Serves 15 • Preparation 30 minutes

HIGH SCHOOL ROCK BIRTHDAY CAKE

2 x basic cakes (see note), baked in 12½ x 8¾ in (32 x 22cm) tins
Basic cream frosting (e.g. page 384) – white, red
Wooden skewers
Silver balls
Sugared jelly sweets for spotlights
Dolls of choice
Prestik® or Blu-tac™

1 Bake the cakes according to the recipe and leave to cool completely.
2 Cut an 8 x 8¾ in (20 x 22cm) rectangle from each cake and sandwich together with frosting to form the stage.
3 Slice the remaining 4¾ x 8¾ in (12 x 22cm) of each section into three 16 x 8¾ in (40 x 22cm) strips. Place three of the strips along the back of the stage for the curtain, sandwiching together with frosting and using wooden skewers to secure. (Freeze the fourth strip for later use in a trifle or similar.)
4 Coat the upper surface of the stage with white frosting and the sides of the cake with red frosting.
5 Coat the curtains with red frosting and use the star or ribbon nozzle to create the drapes. Enhance with silver balls.
6 Position the sugared jelly sweets along the front edge of the stage for spotlights.
7 Attach the dolls to wooden skewers with Prestik® and insert into the cake as illustrated.

Note: You can use a simple cake recipe (e.g. Simple Sponge Cake, page 125) to make the cakes at the dimensions given.

Serves 10 • Preparation 30 minutes

SOCCER WORLD FINAL BIRTHDAY CAKE

1 x batter for basic cake (see note), to be 11 in (28cm) round
1 x batter for basic cake, to be divided and baked in two x 1 quart (1.5 litre)
  ovenproof pudding bowls
Basic cream frosting (e.g. page 384) – green, white, black
Wooden dowel sticks
Toy soccer players

1 Prepare 1 x cake batter. Bake the round cake according to the recipe.

2 Prepare the additional 1 x cake batter. Divide between the two pudding
   bowls and bake for 50–60 minutes until a skewer inserted into the centre
   comes out clean. Leave the cakes to cool completely.

3 With a piping bag, use the multi-hole nozzle and green frosting to coat the
   round cake so that it resemble grass.

4 Use a serrated knife to level the surfaces of the bowl cakes. Cover one with
   a layer of frosting. Upend the second bowl cake and place it on the first, to
   form a ball. Coat the ball with a thin layer of white frosting.

5 Trace templates onto cardboard and mark out the sections on the ball. It is
   easier to decorate the lower section of the ball before placing it in the centre
   of the 'grass', being careful not to disturb the frosting.

6 Use the writing nozzle and black frosting to connect the shapes as
   illustrated, and the star nozzle to decorate the ball.

7 Insert dowel sticks to secure the ball in position before completing the rest
   of the shapes.

8 Place the toy soccer players in position as you like.

**Note: You can use a simple cake recipe (e.g. Simple Sponge Cake, page 125) to make
the cakes at the dimensions given.**

Serves 20 • Preparation 1 hour • Cooking 2 hours

WINNING FORMULA 1 BIRTHDAY CAKE

1 x basic cake (see note), baked in
   12½ x 8¾ in (32 x 22cm) tin
Sugar paste
Powdered food dye – black
Basic cream frosting (e.g. page 384) –
   red, black
Cardboard
Edible glitter
Wooden skewers

1 x chocolate disc or similar, for
   steering wheel
2 x large dome-shaped sugared
   candies
Liquorice strips
4 x round sweets for hubcaps
Wafers
Silver balls

1 Bake the cake according to the recipe and leave to cool completely.

2 Fashion a driver's head (helmet) from a walnut-sized ball of sugar paste and
   set aside to firm up.

3 Dye a small handful of sugar paste black and roll out to ¼ in (4 mm) thick.
   Use templates to cut out desired car decals. Mould a ½ x ¼ in (15 x 5 mm)
   cylinder-shaped piece of sugar paste to support the top wind resistor. Cut
   an oblong strip of black sugar paste for the driver's visor and attach to the
   helmet with a dab of frosting. Set aside to firm up.

4 Use templates and cardboard to cut out wind resistors. Coat the front one
   with red frosting using the star nozzle, while the top and side resistors are
   coated with a thin layer of black frosting. Sprinkle with edible glitter.

5 Cut out cake according to a template. Use a 2 in (5cm) cutter to cut out four
   wheels (refrigerate wheels to make frosting them easier). Use offcuts to
   build up the car behind the driver. Hollow out the cab section slightly.

6 Coat cake with red frosting. Cover wheels with black frosting and attach to
   the body with trimmed wooden skewers. Add sugar paste embellishments.

7 Place the wind resistors in position, pushing the side ones into the cake.

8 Line the cab with a thin layer of red sugar paste. Place the driver's head in
   position, insert the steering wheel and place the candies in position for the
   mirrors. Add the hubcaps.

9 Assemble the top wind resistor by placing a small dab of frosting on one end

of the cylindrical shape to secure the top. Press into position behind head.

10 Use a wooden skewer to add 'vents' alongside the driver's cab.

11 Use liquorice strips to fashion the hood of the car and embellish with a black sugar paste star.

12 Cut the wafer in half along the length, coat with a thin layer of black frosting and cover with a black sugar paste strip. Sprinkle with glitter and place in position at a slight angle to form the tail end of the car.

13 Use silver balls to enhance, as illustrated.

Serves 15 • Preparation 1 hour

Note: You can use a simple cake recipe (e.g. Simple Sponge Cake, page 125) to make the cake at the dimensions given.

FEISTY FIRE ENGINE BIRTHDAY CAKE

2 x basic cakes (see note), baked in 12½ x 8¾ in (32 x 22cm) tins

Sugar paste

Powdered food dye – yellow, red, black

Basic cream frosting (e.g. page 384) – red

1 x clear, disposable, plastic container, measuring approximately 4¼ x 3 in (11 x 8 cm)

2 x toy firefighters

Foil

Liquorice twists

Liquorice strips

Round candies for front and back lights

4 x chocolate discs for wheels

Silver balls

Red and yellow cherries

2 x banana-shaped sweets

Toy fire-fighting tools (optional)

1 Bake the cakes according to the recipe and leave to cool completely.

2 Dye some sugar paste yellow and roll out to ¼ in (4 mm) thick. Fashion a steering wheel, emblems and hubcaps and set aside to firm up.

3 Sandwich the cakes together with a layer of frosting. Cut the upper layer of the cake at an angle to form the front section of the fire engine.

4 Measure the length of the plastic container and trim the sides off the cake accordingly (set aside to use later) so that the cab will fit comfortably across the width of the cake. Coat the truck with red frosting.

5 Cover the toy firefighters' legs with foil and insert into the cab section. Add the steering wheel and place the plastic container over the firefighters. Cover the roof section with frosting and use the star nozzle to add the support sections at each side edge as illustrated.

6 Place the trimmed pieces of cake across the back of the cake to fit neatly behind the cab; coat with red frosting. Fashion a ladder from the liquorice twists and position on top of the truck.

7 Roll some black sugar paste into a sausage; fashion to make the bumpers.

8 Cut liquorice strips into equal lengths and place in position for the front grille. Position the round candies for the front and back lights.

9 Position chocolate discs for wheels, add a hubcap with a dab of frosting and enhance with silver balls, again attaching with a dab of frosting.

10 Roll a liquorice strip into a hosepipe and attach to the side of the fire engine; add a silver ball to the end to simulate the nozzle.

11 Place a row of alternating red and yellow cherries on the roof for flashing emergency lights.

12 Attach the emblems to each panel and enhance with sugar paste stars as illustrated. Attach the banana-shaped sweets for the door handles.

13 Enhance with small fire-fighting tools if using.

Serves 15 • Preparation 1 hour

Note: You can use a simple cake recipe (e.g. Simple Sponge Cake, page 125) to make the cakes at the dimensions given.

Lovely
CUPCAKES

Sweet, dainty, adorable mouthfuls

BUTTER CHOC CUPCAKES

3 eggs
4 oz (125g) butter, softened
1 cup superfine (caster) sugar
½ cup buttermilk
1½ cups self-rising (self-raising) flour,
1 teaspoon cocoa powder
1 teaspoon vanilla extract
½ cup milk chocolate pieces, finely
  chopped

⅓ cup cream

Frosting
1½ cups cup confectioner's (icing)
  sugar
4 oz (125g) butter, softened
5 drops pink food dye
sugar flowers (available from
cake decoration shops)

1 Preheat the oven to 320°F (160°C). Line a 12-cupcake pan with cupcake papers. In a medium-sized bowl, lightly beat the eggs, add butter and sugar, then mix until light and fluffy.

2 Add buttermilk, sifted flour, cocoa powder and vanilla, and stir to combine. Beat with an electric mixer for 2 minutes, until light and creamy. Add chocolate and cream, stir mixture thoroughly.

3 Divide the mixture evenly between the cake papers. Bake for 18–20 minutes until risen and firm to touch. Allow to cool for a few minutes and then transfer to a wire rack. Allow to cool fully before frosting.

4 For the frosting, combine half the confectioner's sugar and butter, mix with a wooden spoon, add remaining confectioner's sugar, butter and food dye and beat with the spoon until light and fluffy. Add frosting to a piping bag and pipe onto cupcakes, then smooth over with spatula and top with flower decorations.

Makes about 12 • Preparation 15 minutes • Cooking 20 minutes

COFFEE MUDS

8 oz (225g) chocolate graham crackers (digestive biscuits)
8 oz (225g) butter, softened
8 oz (225g) semisweet (dark) chocolate
1/3 cup corn (golden) syrup
3 medium eggs, beaten
1/2 teaspoon vanilla extract
1 tablespoon instant coffee

Topping
1¾ oz (50g) white chocolate

1 Preheat the oven to 360°F (180°C). Line a 12-cupcake pan with cupcake papers. Place the graham crackers into a plastic bag, seal, then crush with a rolling pin. Melt 2½ oz (75g) of the butter in a saucepan. Remove from the heat and mix in the cracker crumbs. Divide the graham cracker mixture between the papers, pressing over the base and gently up the sides of each paper. Refrigerate for 20 minutes or until firm.

2 Put the remaining butter, chocolate and syrup into a double boiler. Heat gently, stirring, until melted. Remove from the heat and cool for 5 minutes. Whisk in the eggs, vanilla extract and coffee.

3 Spoon the chocolate mixture over the cracker bases and bake for 20 minutes or until just firm. Leave to cool for 5 minutes.

4 For topping, melt the white chocolate in a double boiler. Drizzle over the cakes.

Makes 12 • Preparation 40 minutes • Cooking 30 minutes

VANILLA CHOC CUPCAKES

3 eggs
4 oz (125g) butter, softened
1 cup superfine (caster) sugar
½ cup vanilla yogurt
1½ cups self-rising (self-raising) flour, sifted
1 tablespoon vanilla extract
3½ oz (100g) semisweet (dark) chocolate pieces

1 tablespoon cocoa powder

Frosting
3½ oz (100g) semisweet (dark) chocolate pieces
20g butter, softened
⅓ cup heavy (double) cream
silver balls (available from cake decoration stores)

1 Preheat the oven to 320°F (160°C). Line a 12-cupcake pan with cupcake papers. In a medium-sized bowl, lightly beat the eggs, add butter and sugar, then mix until light and fluffy.

2 Add yogurt, flour and vanilla, and stir to combine. Add remaining ingredients. Beat with an electric mixer for 2 minutes, until light and creamy.

3 Divide the mixture evenly between the cake papers. Bake for 18–20 minutes until risen and firm to touch. Allow to cool for a few minutes, and then transfer to a wire rack. Allow to cool fully before frosting.

4 Meanwhile, combine the chocolate and butter in a medium-sized saucepan over a medium heat. As the mixture begins to melt, reduce heat to low, stirring constantly, until melted. Remove from heat, add cream, and stir. Rest for 10 minutes: the mixture will be firm and velvety in consistency. Use a fork to apply frosting to each cupcake, and add silver balls to finish.

Makes 12 • Preparation 12 minutes • Cooking 20 minutes

CAFE LATTE CUPCAKES

4 oz (125g) butter, softened
¾ cup milk, scalded then cooled
½ teaspoon vanilla extract
3 eggs
1 cup superfine (caster) sugar
1½ cups self-rising (self-raising) flour
1½ tablespoons non-fat (skim) milk powder
1 tablespoon instant coffee

Frosting
3 cups confectioner's (icing) sugar
1 cup milk powder
1 tablespoon instant coffee
3½ oz (100g) butter, softened
¼ cup milk
4 drops vanilla extract

1 Preheat the oven to 360°F (180°C). Line a 12-cupcake pan with cupcake papers. In a saucepan, heat the butter, ¼ cup of milk and vanilla gently and stir until butter is melted. Add the remaining milk and allow to cool.

2 In a large bowl, whisk the eggs with an electric mixer until thick and creamy. Add the sugar gradually, then stir in half the butter mixture and flour and beat. Add the remaining butter mixture, flour, non-fat milk powder and coffee and beat until smooth.

3 Divide the mixture evenly between the cake papers. Bake for 20 minutes until risen and firm to touch. Allow to cool for a few minutes and then transfer to a wire rack. Allow to cool fully before frosting.

4 Meanwhile, combine all of the ingredients in a medium-sized bowl and beat with an electric mixer to slowly combine for 1 minute. Turn speed up and beat for 5 minutes until combined. Place mixture into a piping bag and pipe onto all cupcakes.

Makes 12 • Preparation 20 minutes • Cooking 20 minutes

LONG MACCHIATO CUPCAKES

½ cup all-purpose (plain) flour
1 cup self-rising (self-raising) flour
4½ tablespoons instant coffee
4 oz (125g) butter, softened
¼ teaspoon vanilla extract
1 cup superfine (caster) sugar
2 eggs
¾ cup water

Frosting

3 cups confectioner's (icing) sugar
1 cup milk powder
1 tablespoon instant coffee
3½ oz (100g) butter, softened
¼ cup milk
4 drops vanilla extract

1 Preheat the oven to 360°F (180°C). Line a 12-cupcake pan with cupcake papers. Sift the dry ingredients together.

2 In a medium-sized bowl, beat the butter, vanilla and sugar with an electric mixer until creamy. Add the eggs one at a time and beat until well combined.

3 Add the dry ingredients to the butter mixture and combine thoroughly, then slowly add the water and mix again.

4 Divide the mixture evenly between the cake papers. Bake for approximately 20 minutes until risen and firm to touch. Allow to cool for a few minutes and then transfer to a wire rack. Allow to cool fully.

5 For the frosting, combine all of the ingredients except the instant coffee in a medium-sized bowl and beat with an electric mixer to slowly combine for 1 minute. Turn speed up and beat until combined. Add 1 teaspoon of water to the coffee and add to the topping, stirring only once. Spread topping evenly onto cupcakes with a teaspoon.

Makes 12 • Preparation 20 minutes • Cooking 20 minutes

BLACK FOREST CUPCAKES

3 eggs
4 oz (125g) butter, softened
1 cup superfine (caster) sugar
½ cup milk
1½ cups self-rising (self-raising) flour
¼ cup cocoa powder
1 tablespoon kirsch liqueur

Frosting
3½ oz (100g) cream
12 fresh cherries
¼ cup chocolate, shaved

1 Preheat the oven to 320°F (160°C). Line a 12-cupcake pan with cupcake papers. In a medium-sized bowl, lightly beat the eggs, add butter and sugar, then mix until light and fluffy.

2 Add milk, sifted flour and cocoa powder, and stir to combine. Beat with an electric mixer for 2 minutes, until light and creamy, then fold through kirsch liqueur.

3 Divide the mixture evenly between the cake papers. Bake for 18–20 minutes until risen and firm to touch. Allow to cool for a few minutes and then transfer to a wire rack. Allow to cool fully before frosting.

4 For the frosting, whip cream until stiff peaks form, then top each cake with a dollop of cream, a sprinkle of chocolate shavings and a fresh cherry.

Makes 12 • Preparation 12 minutes • Cooking 20 minutes

APPLE AND CINNAMON CUPCAKES

½ apple, peeled and chopped into small pieces
juice of 1 lemon
1 tablespoon cinnamon
3 eggs
4 oz (125g) butter, softened
1 cup superfine (caster) sugar
½ cup milk

1½ cups self-rising (self-raising) flour, sifted

Frosting
1½ cups confectioner's (icing) sugar
4 oz (125g) butter, softened
1 tablespoon cinnamon sugar

1 Preheat the oven to 320°F (160°C). Line a 12-cupcake pan with cupcake papers.In a small bowl, coat the apple pieces with lemon juice and sprinkle with cinnamon. In a medium-sized bowl, lightly beat the eggs, add butter and sugar, then mix until light and fluffy.

2 Add milk and flour, and stir to combine. Beat with an electric mixer for 2 minutes, until light and creamy. Add spiced apple and stir through mixture.

3 Divide the mixture evenly between the cake papers. Bake for 18–20 minutes until risen and firm to touch. Allow to cool for a few minutes and then transfer to a wire rack. Allow to cool fully.

4 For frosting, combine half the confectioner's sugar and butter, mix with a wooden spoon, add remaining confectioner's sugar and butter and beat with the spoon until light and fluffy. Spoon topping onto cupcakes and sprinkle cinnamon sugar on top.

Makes 12 • Preparation 12 minutes • Cooking 20 minutes

ORANGE POPPY CUPCAKES

3 eggs
4 oz (125g) butter, softened
1 cup superfine (caster) sugar
½ cup buttermilk
1½ cups self-rising (self-raising) flour
zest of 1 orange
juice of ½ orange
1 teaspoon poppy seeds

Frosting
1½ cups confectioner's (icing) sugar
4 oz (125g) butter, softened
juice of ½ orange
½ teaspoon poppy seeds
zest of 1 orange
candied orange pieces, cut into thin
  slivers

1 Preheat the oven to 320°F (160°C). Line a 12-cupcake pan with cupcake papers. In a medium-sized bowl, lightly beat the eggs, add butter and sugar, then mix until light and fluffy.

2 Add buttermilk and sifted flour, and stir to combine. Beat with an electric mixer for 2 minutes, until light and creamy. Add orange zest, orange juice and poppy seeds, and mix through with a wooden spoon.

3 Divide the mixture evenly between the cake cases. Bake for 18–20 minutes until risen and firm to touch. Allow to cool for a few minutes and then transfer to a wire rack. Allow to cool fully before frosting.

4 Meanwhile, combine topping ingredients except candied orange, and mix with a wooden spoon. Spoon onto cakes. Top with candied orange pieces.

Makes 12 • Preparation 12 minutes • Cooking 20 minutes

DECORATED CUPCAKES

4 oz (125g) butter or margarine
1 teaspoon vanilla extract
¾ cup superfine (caster) sugar
2 eggs
2 cups self-rising (self-raising) flour
pinch of salt
⅔ cup milk

Frosting
3 cups confectioner's (icing) sugar
green and pink food dye
glacé cherries

1 Preheat oven to 360°F (180°C).

2 Beat butter, vanilla extract and sugar together in a bowl until light and fluffy. Add eggs one at a time, beating well after each addition.

3 Sift flour and salt together, add to the creamed mixture alternately with milk, stirring until smooth and all ingredients are well combined.

4 Spoon about 1 tablespoon of mixture into each paper patty case or buttered patty pans. Bake for 15 minutes or until golden brown. Remove from oven and cool on a wire rack.

5 Sift confectioner's sugar into a bowl, add sufficient hot water to make a smooth, spreadable frosting. Keep a small amount aside and dye it green. Add pink dye to the rest. Quickly spread pink frosting over each cake and decorate with green frosting and glacé cherries.

Makes about 24 • Preparation 30 minutes • Cooking 15 minutes

BUTTERFLY CUPCAKES

3 eggs
4 oz (125g) butter, softened
1 cup superfine (caster) sugar
½ cup milk
1½ cups self-rising (self-raising) flour, sifted
1 teaspoon vanilla extract

Frosting
1½ cups confectioner's (icing) sugar
1 teaspoon vanilla extract
4 oz (125g) butter, softened

1 Preheat the oven to 320°F (160°C). Line a 12-cupcake pan with cupcake papers. In a medium-sized bowl, lightly beat the eggs, add butter and sugar, then mix until light and fluffy.

2 Add milk, flour and vanilla, and stir to combine. Beat with an electric mixer for 2 minutes, until light and creamy.

3 Divide the mixture evenly between the cake papers. Bake for 18–20 minutes until risen and firm to touch. Allow to cool for a few minutes and then transfer to a wire rack. Allow to cool fully.

4 For frosting, combine all topping ingredients, mix with a wooden spoon until well combined, then beat with the spoon until light and fluffy.

5 Place mixture into a piping bag, and set aside. Using a sharp knife, cut a circle into the centre of each cupcake, slicing the top off. Cut these circles in half and set aside. Fill the centre of each cupcake with frosting, and stand the two half-circles of cake upright, to form wings.

Makes about 12 • Preparation 12 minutes • Cooking 20 minutes

VANILLA RUDOLPH CUPCAKES

3 eggs
4 oz (125g) butter, softened
1 cup superfine (caster) sugar
½ cup milk
1½ cups self-rising (self-raising) flour, sifted
2 teaspoons vanilla extract

Frosting
3½ oz (100g) semisweet (dark) chocolate
1 tablespoon butter, softened
⅓ cup heavy (double) cream
novelty reindeers (available from specialist cake decoration stores)

1 Preheat the oven to 320°F (160°C). Line a 12-cupcake pan with cupcake papers. In a medium-sized bowl, lightly beat the eggs, add butter and sugar, then mix until light and fluffy.

2 Add milk, flour and vanilla, and stir to combine. Beat with an electric mixer for 2 minutes, until light and creamy.

3 Divide the mixture evenly between the cake papers. Bake for 18–20 minutes until risen and firm to touch. Allow to cool for a few minutes and then transfer to a wire rack. Allow to cool fully before frosting.

4 Meanwhile, combine the chocolate and butter in a medium-sized saucepan over medium heat. As the mixture begins to melt, reduce heat to low, and add cream slowly, stirring constantly until the mixture thickens. Remove from heat and cool. Decorate the top of each cake with topping and a novelty reindeer.

Makes about 12 • Preparation 12 minutes • Cooking 20 minutes

CHAI TEA CUPCAKES

¼ cup hot water
¼ cup chai mixture (Indian spiced tea)
3 eggs
4 oz (125g) butter, softened
1 cup superfine (caster) sugar
¼ cup milk
1½ cups self-rising (self-raising) flour
1 teaspoon vanilla extract

1 teaspoon cinnamon
1 teaspoon nutmeg

Frosting
¼ cup raw sugar
2 tablespoons warm water
cinnamon sugar
12 star anises

1 Preheat the oven to 320°F (160°C). Line a 12-cupcake pan with cupcake papers. In a small bowl, add hot water to the spiced tea mixture, stand for 15 minutes, strain and set aside. In a medium-sized bowl, lightly beat the eggs, add butter and sugar, then mix until light and fluffy.

2 Add milk and sifted flour, and stir to combine. Add remaining ingredients. Beat with an electric mixer for 2 minutes, until light and creamy. Add chai tea and stir through.

3 Divide the mixture evenly between the cake papers. Bake for 18–20 minutes until risen and firm to touch. Allow to cool for a few minutes and then transfer to a wire rack. Allow to cool fully before frosting.

4 For the frosting, combine the raw sugar and water in a small bowl, mix with a wooden spoon, spoon onto cupcakes and sprinkle with cinnamon sugar. Decorate each cupcake with a single star anise.

Makes about 12 • Preparation 12 minutes • Cooking 20 minutes

DOUBLE WHITE CUPCAKES

3 eggs
4 oz (125g) butter, softened
1 cup superfine (caster) sugar
½ cup milk
1½ cups self-rising (self-raising) flour, sifted
3½ oz (100g) white chocolate, grated
1 teaspoon vanilla extract

Frosting
1½ cups confectioner's (icing) sugar
4 oz (125g) butter, softened
72 pre-made meringue decorations (with silver balls)

1 Preheat the oven to 320°F (160°C). Line a 12-cupcake pan with cupcake
   papers. In a medium-sized bowl, lightly beat the eggs, add butter and sugar,
   then mix until light and fluffy.

2 Add the milk, flour, chocolate and vanilla, and stir to combine. Beat with an
   electric mixer for 2 minutes, until light and creamy.

3 Divide the mixture evenly between the cake papers. Bake for 18–20 minutes
   until risen and firm to touch. Allow to cool for a few minutes and then
   transfer to a wire rack. Allow to cool fully.

4 Combine the confectioner's sugar and butter; beat with a wooden spoon
   until light and fluffy. Spoon frosting onto cupcakes, add decorations.

Makes about 12 • Preparation 12 minutes • Cooking 20 minutes

VANILLA ROSE CUPCAKES

3 eggs
4 oz (125g) butter, softened
1 cup superfine (caster) sugar
½ cup milk
1½ cups self-rising (self-raising) flour, sifted
1 teaspoon vanilla extract

Frosting
1½ cups confectioner's (icing) sugar
1 teaspoon rose water
4 oz (125g) butter, softened
6 drops vanilla extract
miniature dried roses, approximately 8 per cupcake
  (available from specialty cake decoration stores)

1 Preheat the oven to 320°F (160°C). Line a 12-cupcake pan with cupcake papers. In a medium-sized bowl, lightly beat the eggs, add butter and sugar, then mix until light and fluffy.

2 Add milk, flour and vanilla, and stir to combine. Beat with an electric mixer for 2 minutes, until light and creamy.

3 Divide the mixture evenly between the cake papers. Bake for 18–20 minutes until risen and firm to touch. Allow to cool for a few minutes and then transfer to a wire rack. Allow to cool fully.

4 For the frosting, combine half of all the topping ingredients, except roses. Mix with a wooden spoon, add remaining ingredients and beat with the spoon until light and fluffy. Place mixture into a piping bag with a plain nozzle and pipe onto cupcakes. Decorate with roses.

Makes about 12 • Preparation 12 minutes • Cooking 20 minutes

LAVENDER CUPCAKES

3 eggs
4 oz (125g) butter, softened
1 cup superfine (caster) sugar
½ cup milk
1½ cups self-rising (self-raising) flour,
 sifted
1 teaspoon vanilla extract

Frosting
1½ cups confectioner's (icing) sugar
1 teaspoon lavender extract
4 oz (125g) butter, softened
2 drops purple food dye
candied lavender (available from cake
 decoration stores)

1 Preheat the oven to 320°F (160°C). Line a 12-cupcake pan with cupcake papers. In a medium-sized bowl, lightly beat the eggs, add butter and sugar, then mix until light and fluffy.

2 Add milk, flour and vanilla, and stir to combine. Beat with an electric mixer for 2 minutes, until light and creamy.

3 Divide the mixture evenly between the cake papers. Bake for 18–20 minutes until risen and firm to touch. Allow to cool for a few minutes and then transfer to a wire rack. Allow to cool fully before frosting.

4 For frosting, combine half the topping ingredients except candied lavender, mix with a wooden spoon, add remaining ingredients and beat with a whisk until light and fluffy.

5 Apply the topping with the back of a teaspoon or a small spatula. Place the candied lavender on top.

Makes about 12 • Preparation 12 minutes • Cooking 20 minutes

COFFEE AND WALNUT CUPCAKES

9 oz (250g) butter, at room
  temperature
½ cup sugar
2 eggs
2 tablespoons Baileys Irish Cream
1 cup chopped walnuts
2 tablespoons instant coffee powder

1½ cups self-rising (self-raising) flour
confectioner's (icing) sugar

Sauce
½ cup superfine (caster) sugar
1 cup heavy (double) cream
1 tablespoon instant coffee powder

1 Preheat oven to 360°F (180°C).

2 Beat butter and sugar until light and fluffy, stir in eggs, Baileys and walnuts.
  Sift in coffee and flour and mix to combine.

3 Divide mixture evenly into a lightly buttered 12-hole muffin or friand tin.

4 Bake for 15–20 minutes or until risen and firm. Leave to cool for 10 minutes,
  then remove from tin.

5 Meanwhile, to make the sauce, heat sugar and ¼ cup water in saucepan
  until mixture is boiling and sugar dissolves. Reduce heat, simmer until
  golden. Add cream and coffee. Bring to the boil and simmer until toffee
  dissolves and sauce thickens.

6 Pour sauce over cake. Serve with tea or coffee and Irish cream liqueur.

Makes 12 • Preparation 20 minutes • Cooking 20 minutes

STICKY DATE CUPCAKES

2 eggs
4½ oz (135g) butter, at room temperature
¾ cup superfine (caster) sugar
1 cup self-rising (self-raising) flour
14 oz (400g) dates, chopped
2 teaspoons instant coffee powder
1 teaspoon baking soda (bicarbonate of soda)
1 teaspoon vanilla extract

1 cup ground almond flour
½ cup walnuts, finely chopped

Frosting

1 cup light-brown sugar, firmly packed
2 oz (60g) unsalted butter
1 teaspoon vanilla extract
1 cup whipped cream
12 dates

1 Preheat the oven to 320°F (160°C). Line a 12-cupcake pan with cupcake papers. In a medium bowl, lightly beat the eggs, add the butter and sugar, then mix until light and fluffy.

2 Add ¾ cup water and the sifted flour, and stir to combine. Add remaining ingredients. Mix with a wooden spoon for 2 minutes, until light and creamy.

3 Divide the mixture evenly between the cake papers. Bake for 18–20 minutes until risen and firm to touch. Allow to cool for a few minutes and then transfer to a wire rack. Allow to cool fully.

4 For the frosting, combine sugar, butter, vanilla and 1 tablespoon water in a saucepan. Bring to a simmer over medium-low heat, stirring constantly. Without stirring again, simmer for 1 minute. Remove from heat and allow to cool. Fold through whipped cream. Spoon onto cupcakes and top with dates.

Makes 12 • Preparation 12 minutes • Cooking 20 minutes

Frosting and FILLINGS

Finishing touches are the loveliest touches

Fudge frosting

4 oz (125g) butter or margarine
1 cup brown sugar, lightly packed
½ cup heavy (double) cream

1 Beat butter or margarine and brown sugar together in a bowl until light and creamy in tone, about 5 minutes.
2 Gradually add cream, beating well after each addition. Continue beating until a thick consistency is obtained.

Covers a 9 in (23cm) cake

Butter cream frosting

4½ oz (125g) butter
1½ cups confectioner's (icing) sugar

1 Cream together butter and sifted sugar until light and fluffy. Add from the list below as desired, and beat thoroughly.

Vanilla: 1 teaspoon vanilla extract and 1 teaspoon water

Peppermint: 1 teaspoon peppermint extract, 1 teaspoon water

Orange: 1 teaspoon orange juice and 1 teaspoon grated orange zest

Sherry: 2 teaspoons sherry

Chocolate: Sift 1 tablespoon cocoa powder with the confectioner's sugar and 1 teaspoon vanilla extract.

Covers an 8 in (20cm) cake

Passionfruit glaze

1 cup confectioner's (icing) sugar
1½ tablespoons passionfruit pulp (canned or fresh)

1 Place sifted confectioner's sugar into a mixing bowl. Add enough passionfruit pulp to make a smooth, spreadable glaze.

Covers an 8 in (20cm) cake

Caramel frosting

1½ cups brown sugar, sifted
2 tablespoons milk
1 oz (30g) butter

1 Combine all ingredients in a small, heavy-based saucepan. Slowly bring to the boil, stirring constantly.
2 Remove from heat and beat until creamy. Using a wet palette knife, spread the frosting over the cake.

Covers an 8 in (20cm) cake

Butterscotch frosting

1½ cups brown sugar
¼ cup milk
1 oz (30g) butter
1 cup confectioner's (icing) sugar

1 Place sugar, milk and butter in a saucepan and cook over a low heat, stirring constantly, until sugar dissolves. Bring to the boil and boil for 3–4 minutes. Remove from heat

and set aside to cool until just warm, then beat in confectioner's sugar until frosting is of a spreadable consistency. Use immediately.

Covers a 8 in (20cm) cake

Glacé icing

1 cup confectioner's (icing) sugar
1 teaspoon butter
few drops of vanilla extract

1 Place sifted confectioner's sugar in a heat-proof bowl over a pan of simmering water.

2 Make a well in the centre of confectioner's sugar, add butter, vanilla extract and 1 tablespoon boiling water, and stir slowly until all confectioner's sugar has been incorporated and icing is smooth and shiny. Use while still warm.

3 For variations, try:

Chocolate: Add 2 tablespoons sifted cocoa powder to confectioner's sugar and an extra 1 teaspoon boiling water.

Coffee: Add 1 teaspoon coffee powder to the confectioner's sugar.

Orange: Add 1 tablespoon fresh orange juice instead of boiling water and ½ teaspoon orange zest.

Lemon: Add 1 tablespoon lemon juice instead of boiling water and ½ teaspoon lemon zest.

Covers the top of an 8 in (20cm) cake or 12 patty cakes

Cream cheese frosting

8 oz (250g) cream cheese
1½ cups confectioner's (icing) sugar
½ teaspoon vanilla extract
1 teaspoon lemon juice

1 Beat cream cheese until soft, add sifted confectioner's sugar, vanilla extract and lemon juice, continue beating until smooth and creamy. If mixture is a little too soft to spread, refrigerate until firmer.

Covers an 11 x 7 in (28 x 18cm) rectangular cake

Chestnut filling

2 teaspoons instant coffee powder
8 oz (250g) canned, sweetened chestnut purée
13 oz (370g) ricotta cheese, crumbled
3 tablespoons coffee liqueur

1 Dissolve coffee powder in ½ cup hot water.

2 Place chestnut purée in a bowl, add the crumbled ricotta, dissolved coffee and coffee liqueur. Beat together until mixture is smooth and of a spreading consistency.

Fills two 8 in (20cm) cakes

Peppermint glaze

2 tablespoons gelatin
2 tablespoons lemon juice, strained
1 egg white
1½ cups confectioner's (icing) sugar
few drops peppermint extract
few drops green food dye

1 Sprinkle gelatin over ¼ cup boiling water and beat briskly with a fork until gelatin has dissolved. Allow to cool but not set, then add lemon juice, mixing well.

2 In a small bowl, beat egg whites until stiff peaks form.

3 Gradually add gelatin mixture, beating well to combine.

4 Add sifted confectioner's sugar and beat until thick and glossy.

5 Add peppermint extract to taste and sufficient green food dye to give the glaze a pale green shade.

Covers a 9 in (23cm) cake

Fondant

Fondant can be bought in supermarkets or you can make your own with this easy recipe.

2 lb (1kg) pure confectioner's (icing) sugar
1 tablespoon gelatin
½ cup liquid glucose
1 tablespoon glycerine

1 Sift confectioner's sugar into a large bowl.

2 Put ¼ cup water in a small saucepan and sprinkle with the gelatin. Cook over low heat, stirring until dissolved. Do not allow to boil. Remove from the heat, add the glucose and glycerine, stir until the glucose dissolves. Allow to cool.

3 Make a well in the centre of the confectioner's sugar, gradually pour in three–quarters of the liquid and mix to form a firm dough. If the fondant is too dry, add a little of the remaining liquid. If the fondant seems too soft, add a little more confectioner's sugar.

4 Turn out onto a clean work surface dusted with a little cornstarch and knead until smooth and satiny.

5 Wrap in cling film until ready to use.

Covers an 8 in (20cm) round cake

Orange butter cream frosting

7 oz (200g) butter
3 cups confectioner's (icing) sugar, sifted
2 teaspoons orange juice
zest of ½ orange

1 Beat butter until soft, add confectioner's sugar, orange juice and zest and continue beating until light and fluffy.

Covers an 8 in (20cm) cake

Almond paste topping

18 oz (500g) pure confectioner's (icing) sugar, sifted
4½ oz (125g) ground almonds or marzipan meal
2 egg yolks
2 tablespoons sweet sherry
a squeeze of lemon juice

1 In a large bowl, combine the almond or marzipan meal with the confectioner's sugar. Make a well in the centre.

2 Combine egg yolks, sherry and lemon juice. Add the liquid to the dry ingredients gradually. Combine to a firm paste. If too moist, add extra confectioner's sugar; if too dry, add extra sherry and lemon juice.

3 Knead lightly but do not handle too much or it will become sticky. Wrap in cling wrap until ready to use

Covers an 8 in (20cm) cake

After covering the cake with almond paste, it is important to leave the cake covered with baking paper in a cool, dry place for 3–7 days. This will dry the surface of the almond paste so that when the fondant is put on, no almond oil will seep through and stain the fondant. If time is short, you can brush over the almond paste with lightly beaten egg white and leave for 24 hours only before putting on the fondant

Pineapple filling

1 tablespoon gelatin
15 oz (425g) canned, crushed pineapple
½ cup sugar
juice of 1 lemon
1¼ cups heavy (double) cream

1 Dissolve gelatin in ½ cup boiling water, cool slightly.

2 Mix together undrained pineapple, sugar and lemon juice in a bowl. Add cooled gelatin and mix well. Place in refrigerator until mixture is just beginning to set around the edge.

3 Whip cream until thick and fold into gelatin mixture. Chill until thick enough to spread. Do not chill for too long or the mixture will set

Fills an 8 in (20cm) cake

Chocolate ripple cream

3½ oz (100g) semisweet (dark) chocolate
1 cup heavy (double) cream, well chilled and whipped

1 Melt chocolate in a small bowl set over a saucepan of simmering water. Fold melted chocolate into chilled cream.

Fills and tops an 8 in (20cm) cake

Mock cream frosting

7 oz (200g) butter, cut into cubes
¾ cup superfine (caster) sugar
½ teaspoon vanilla extract

1 Place butter and sugar in a mixing bowl, beat until light and fluffy, about 5 minutes.

2 Add 1 cup cold water and continue beating for about 1 minute.

3 Pour off as much water as possible from mixture. Beat again until smooth, add another cup of cold water and repeat process, pouring off all of the water.

4 Add vanilla extract and continue beating until mixture is light and creamy. Spread over cake or use as a filling. Use same day. Do not refrigerate or mock cream will separate.

Covers an 8 in (20cm) cake

Vanilla butter cream frosting

7 oz (200g) butter, cubed
3 cups confectioner's (icing) sugar, sifted
1 teaspoon vanilla extract

1 Beat butter until soft and creamy, add confectioner's sugar and vanilla extract, continue beating until white and creamy.

Covers an 8 in (20cm) cake

Crème pâtissière filling

1 cup milk
½ teaspoon vanilla extract
⅓ cup superfine (caster) sugar
3 egg yolks
2 tablespoons cornstarch (cornflour)

1 Heat milk and vanilla in a heavy-based saucepan until boiling.

2 Beat the sugar and eggs together in a bowl until the mixture is thick and creamy and leaves a distinct trail when the beaters are lifted out of the mixture. Fold in the cornstarch.

3 Pour the hot milk onto the egg mixture, beating well. Return the mixture to the pan and reheat, stirring constantly. Boil for 1 minute, then pour into a bowl and cover with a sheet of baking paper until ready to use.

Makes 1 cup

Lemon filling

4 egg yolks
½ cup sugar
¼ cup lemon juice
finely grated zest of 1 lemon
1 tablespoon cream

1 Place egg yolks and sugar in the top of a double boiler, beat over simmering water until smooth.

2 Add lemon juice and lemon zest and continue stirring until mixture thickens, about 5 minutes.

3 Remove from heat, add cream and mix well. Chill until firm enough to spread.

Fills an 8 in (20cm) cake

Classic creamy frosting

2 cups sugar
pinch of cream of tartar
2 egg whites, stiffly beaten

1 Place sugar in a saucepan with 1 cup water and stir over low heat until sugar has dissolved. Bring to boil without stirring, and heat until a small amount of syrup dropped in cold water forms a soft ball.

2 Remove from the heat, add the cream of tartar and beat until the syrup is cloudy.

3 Pour onto the stiffly beaten egg whites, beating all the time. Keep beating until the frosting thickens and loses its shiny appearance.

4 Add extracts and food dye of your choice. Use immediately.

Covers an 8 in (20cm) cake

Royal icing glaze

26½ oz (750g) pure confectioner's (icing) sugar
3 egg whites, at room temperature
½ teaspoon acetic acid or 1 teaspoon lemon juice

1 Sift confectioner's sugar through a fine sieve onto a large square of baking paper.

2 Break egg whites into a mixing bowl and beat lightly until frothy.

3 Using a wooden spoon, gradually beat in about half the quantity of sifted confectioner's sugar. Beat each addition in well before adding the next. Continue beating until the mixture becomes light and fluffy (about 5–10 minutes).

4 Add acetic acid or lemon juice and remaining confectioner's sugar, stirring in a little at a time. Sufficient confectioner's sugar has been added when the glaze holds up in peaks on the spoon – the quantity will vary depending on the volume of egg white. If you leave the glaze at any time during beating, cover with damp cloth to prevent a crust forming on the top.

Covers an 8 in (20cm) cake

These gorgeous decorative flourishes will add that certain je ne sais quoi. Impressive to behold (and surprisingly easy to pull off), these fine finishes will have you slapping greedy hands away and basking in the admiration of wide-eyed family, friends and guests.

Chocolate curls

1 Have a block or long piece of chocolate at room temperature. If the weather is hot, you may need to refrigerate for 30 minutes. Run a potato peeler firmly down the side of chocolate block to form curl. Gently remove curl from peeler. Keep on a plate in a cool place until needed.

Spun sugar

1 cup sugar
pinch of cream of tartar

1 Place sugar, cream of tartar and ½ cup water in a small saucepan. Heat gently, stirring constantly until the sugar dissolves.

2 Raise heat, bring to the boil without stirring. Using a wet pastry brush, remove undissolved sugar crystals from the side of the saucepan. Boil until toffee becomes golden. Remove from heat and cool slightly.

3 Coat the back of two wooden spoons with toffee, place them back to back and gently pull apart.

4 As thread of toffee is formed, continue bringing spoons together and apart until the toffee starts to set and threads have formed.

5 Place the toffee threads over a cake or pastry, or use for, e.g., croquembouche. Repeat the process until all the toffee is used.

Crazy coconut

1 Place required amount of coconut on a small plate or saucer. Add food dye, drop by drop, to coconut, pressing and tossing with a skewer until all coconut is well-dyed. Leave to dry for about 1 hour.

Toffee strawberries

1 cup sugar
8 oz (250g) strawberries

1 Place the sugar and ⅔ cup water in a saucepan. Dissolve the sugar over a low heat.

2 Wipe and hull strawberries and place on a wire rack.

3 When sugar has dissolved, raise heat. Boil without stirring for about 8 minutes or until syrup is thick.

4 Remove from heat and stand the pan in cold water for 2 minutes.

5 Place a strawberry on the tip of a skewer and dip into glaze, coating completely.

6 Hold strawberry over the pan until excess syrup has drained away. Cool on a buttered wire rack until firm. Repeat with remaining strawberries.

Fanned strawberries

1 Wash strawberries and pat dry, leaving stalks intact. Cut strawberry from bottom toward the stalk with paring knife, being careful not to cut right through – leave just enough to hold it together. Make the slices very thin.

2 Gently push slices apart to form a semi-circle. Fanned strawberries can be glazed with warm jelly for added effect.

Lattice work

1 A decorative lattice can be made with glacé icing (page 385) or whipped cream (glacé icing should be soft, but not runny). Spoon into a piping bag fitted with a writing or very small, plain tube. Twist the top of bag to seal. Use one hand to steady the bag and the other to press the top of the bag to extrude icing or cream. Pipe toward you with even pressure and movement.

2 Complete by piping across cake. If edges are messy, trim with a small, sharp knife.

Marzipan fruits

7 oz (200g) roll marzipan
whole cloves
assorted food dye

1 Knead marzipan lightly until pliable. Keep covered with a damp cloth to prevent drying while making each shape.

2 Dust hands lightly with cornstarch, then pull off hazelnut-sized pieces of marzipan from the roll.

To shape a pear: Roll into a cone and mould into a plump pear shape. Press the star end of a clove into the base of the pear and the tip of the clove into the top to look like a stalk.

To shape an apple: Roll into a ball; press a clove into top and bottom.

To shape an orange: Roll marzipan into ball. Roll over fine surface of a grater to create effect of citrus rind.

To shape a lemon and lime: Form into an oval shape, pinch points and roll over fine surface of a grater to create effect of citrus rind.

To shape a peach: Roll into ball, use skewer to mark dent for the cheeks.

To paint fruit: Blend diluted food dyes to appropriate shades. Using a fine paint brush, paint the fruit. Create realistic effects by brushing a second shade over the first one after it has dried – for example, the blush on a peach or the green spot at the blossom end of an orange or lemon.

Chocolate logs

1 Melt cooking chocolate in top of a double boiler or in a heatproof bowl over simmering water. Do not allow the water to touch the bowl. Stir occasionally until melted and smooth.

2 Using a metal spatula, spread melted chocolate thinly and evenly over a marble slab or flat glass plate. Smooth surface as much as possible, then allow to set slightly or until chocolate no longer looks wet.

3 While chocolate is still supple, hold a spatula or egg lifter at an angle and push lightly forward about 1 in (2.5cm) or until chocolate forms a log. Repeat until all chocolate is used.

Glacé feathers

1 Make up quantity of white glacé icing (page 385). Make second quantity in bright, contrasting shade. Using a palette knife, spread white icing quickly and evenly over cake.

2 Spoon contrasting shade into a piping bag fitted with a writing tube. Pipe straight lines across cake, leaving 1 in (2.5cm) between each line. Drag a skewer or tip of a knife across cake at right angles to the piped lines.

3 Turn cake around and drag the skewer in between the first lines in the opposite direction to give the feathered effect. Allow icing to set before moving the cake.

Piping a shell border

1 Beat heavy cream in a chilled bowl until thick. Spoon cream into a piping bag fitted with a star tube. Twist top of the bag to seal.

2 Start close to the edge of the cake, forcing cream out by applying pressure to top of the bag with your right hand. Other hand should be close to the tube to guide it. As cream comes out of the tube, slightly push it backwards, then raise bag up and down. Start the next shell where last one finished.

Frosted fruits or flowers

1 Choose selection of fruit, such as strawberries, grapes or mandarin segments, or flowers, such as violets or rose petals. For the frosting, you will need egg whites and superfine sugar.

2 Place 2–3 egg whites in small bowl. Beat lightly with a fork to break the egg white up slightly. Pour about ½ cup superfine sugar into another bowl, then place baking paper on a flat tray or board and sprinkle with a little extra superfine sugar over the paper. Dip violet, mint leaf or fruit into the egg white, shaking off any excess, then coat quickly

and lightly with the sugar. Place on the paper to dry.

3 Reshape the flowers if necessary. Continue frosting the remaining flowers, fruit and leaves. Arrange in petits fours cases or on a serving plate.

Praline

½ cup sugar
½ teaspoon white vinegar
2½ oz (75g) almonds, chopped

1 Combine sugar, 2 tablespoons water and vinegar in a small saucepan. Stir over low heat until sugar dissolves. Bring to the boil without stirring and cook for about 5 minutes or until golden brown.

2 Add almonds and quickly pour onto lightly buttered baking tray. Allow to set, break into pieces and either finely crush in a food processor or place in a plastic bag and crush with a rolling pin. Store in an airtight jar and use as required.

Toasted flaked almonds

1 Spread 9 oz (250g) slivered almonds thinly onto a baking sheet. Bake in a preheated oven at 360°F (180°C) for 4 minutes. Remove the baking sheet and use a spatula to turn the almonds.

2 Return to the oven and bake for another 4 minutes. Remove and turn again. Continue until the almonds are a golden brown. Allow to cool on the baking sheet. When cool, press around the sides of a cake covered with glaze or cream.

Covers a 9 in (23cm) cake

Chocolate leaves

1 Heat cooking chocolate in the top of a double boiler or a heatproof bowl over a pan of simmering water, stirring until chocolate has melted. Cool the chocolate quickly by pouring into a small bowl.

2 Wash and dry leaves well. Dip one side of each leaf in the chocolate, lightly shaking off any excess. You may wish to paint the chocolate on to one side of the leaves using a small paint brush.

3 Place leaves green-side down on a sheet of baking paper or foil, allow to dry at room temperature. When the chocolate has set, gently peel leaves away and discard. Lift the chocolate leaves onto the cake using a knife as the heat of your hands may melt the chocolate.

Recipe Index

First published in 2013 by
New Holland Publishers
London • Sydney • Cape Town • Auckland
www.newhollandpublishers.com

Garfield House 86–88 Edgware Road London W2 2EA United Kingdom
1/66 Gibbes Street Chatswood NSW 2067 Australia
Wembley Square First Floor Solan Road Gardens Cape Town 8001 South Africa
218 Lake Road Northcote Auckland New Zealand

A catalogue record of this book is available at the British Library and at the National
Library of Australia.

ISBN: 9781742573847

10 9 8 7 6 5 4 3 2 1

Managing director: Fiona Schultz
Publisher: Fiona Schultz
Project editor: Kate Sherington
Designer: Lorena Susak
Production director: Olga Dementiev
Printer: Toppan Leefung Printing Limited

Follow New Holland Publishers on
Facebook: www.facebook.com/NewHollandPublishers

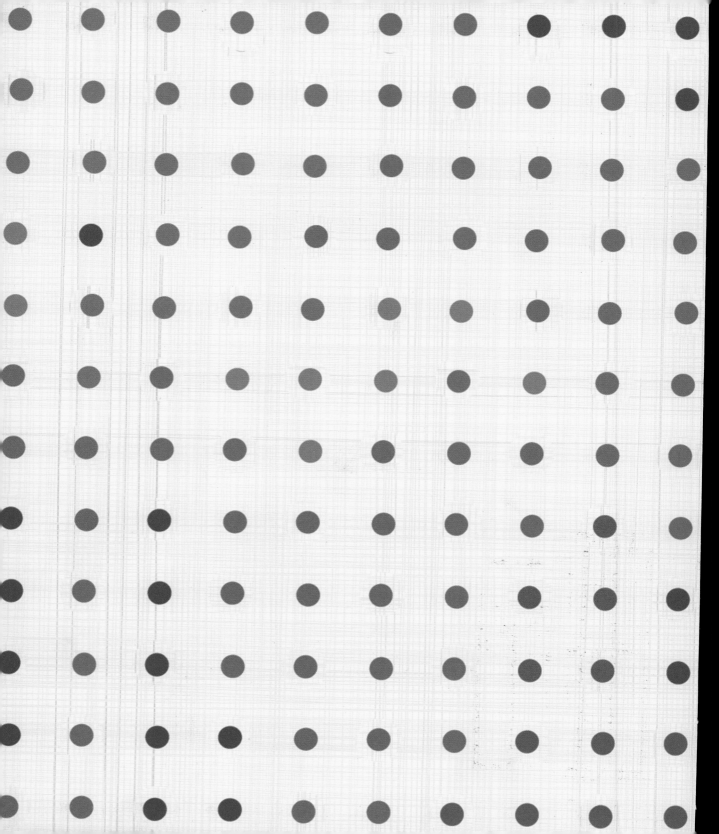